FOLLOW THE LIGHT OF TRUTH

Back To Zion

YOUR WORD IS TRUTH

By

Thomas O. Aladi

PROISLE PUBLISHING

Proisle Publishing Services LLC
Simply Best Reads Bookstore
39-67, 58th Street 1st Floor
Woodside NY 11377
Phone: (+1 347-922-3779)
info@proislepublishing.com

ISBN: 978-1-959449-96-6

How to get the best benefit out of this book.

Dear reader.

The author suggests that you read and study the information presented in this book along with the bible references. Read and meditate on the things written. Examining the topic presentations in this book with what is written in the bible will help you the reader to appreciate and act on the accuracy of understanding presented in this book.

(Isaiah 54:13, Proverbs 1:23). Our God will teach all his chosen ones using his Holy Spirit that He pours out for his chosen people. The author only made summary and explanations of the presented scriptures. You the reader who is seeking the favor of the God of Israel, will search out these scriptures until you gain the true knowledge of Him and his activities. Acquiring the knowledge of the true God of Israel and his son will mean everlasting life to all who will diligently search for Him (John 17:3).

"A thousand will fall at your side and ten thousand at your right hand, but to you it will not come near. 8 You will only see it with your eyes as you witness the punishment of the wicked. 9 Because you said: "Yahuwah is my refuge," You have made the Most High your dwelling; 10 No disaster will befall you, And no plague will come near your tent. 11 For he will give his angels a command concerning you, to guard you in all your ways." (Psalms 91:7-11).

Abbreviations as used in this book.

Abbreviations are used in this book to reference books of the bible. The first three or four letters were used when referencing each book of the bible as in examples below.

Gen 3:1-5 = Genesis chapter 3 verses 1 through 5.
Exo = Exodus.
Lev = Leviticus.
Num = Numbers.
Deut = Deuteronomy.
1Pt 3:8 = 1st Peter chapter 3 verse 8.
ETC.

Introduction

In my first book "The road leading back to Zion: Homecoming for Abraham's chosen off springs". I was led by the spirit of God to present scriptural evidences proving that the chosen race, the ones serving the will or punishment from their God is not the European white nations but rather it is the negroes black race that is serving the punishment and slavery imposed on them by God (Jer25:14,Isaiah 14:1-3). The spirit also led me since no man can understand the hidden things of the true God except when He reveals it using his Holy Spirit sent from above. The promised Holy spirit helps us in discerning and understanding accurately the words of our father in heaven, the things He has promised long ago, which things He is now ready to bring to completion (Pro 1:23).

The second book, "Extra Oil for your lamps" continued to build on the truth and accuracy of the revealed things of our God by the Holy Spirit. The accurate understanding of these things written in the bible long ago is been revealed so that the weary pilgrims of Israel, the chosen ones can follow the light of our God's word and endure until the end.

In this third book "Follow the light of God's word back to Zion" The Holy Spirit continues to encourage and strengthen the chosen ones to hope in Yahuwah our God (Ps 37:34) and trust in His appointed times (Eccl 3:1-8). He will carry out all his

promises to return and search for His sheep and rescue them from the one stronger than them, and from the hands of thieves and plunderers (Ezek 34:1-5. Ps 142:6, Jer 31:11, John 10:8).
So keep your faith and hope strong in the salvation ready for revealing in the last day of our punishment and tribulation (Isa 45:25, 1pt 1:3-5, Isa 46:13).

Peoples of other nations who fear and want to worship the true God of Israel, should rejoice with the chosen ones of Israel in the things our God is accomplishing for the sanctification of His holy name in all the earth (Ezek 39:7-8, Deut 32:43, Zech 8:22-23).

Table of content

Follow the light of truth

God's word will shine as a lamp for your feet, showing you where we are standing at the moment in our journey among the nations. And as a light it will illuminate to show you how far more we have to endure as we travel the path of our God's judgment on our way back to Zion. We need to study the written words of our God if we want it's light guide us .

How to walk by the light of truth when Yahuwah the God of Israel awakens you.

Ezek 37:1-14. Yahuwah our God foretold that He will pour out his spirit to awaken his chosen people (the whole house of Israel) from being dead as a nation to come to life in the final part of their days of punishment. Now that He has awakened you or is about to awaken you, how should you walk with your God after you are fully awakened from the dead?

Here is how and the things you need to know.

Isa 8:19-20, Exod 20:1-6. We the awakened people of Israel should seek and call on the name of Yahuwah our God and stop calling on the false gods of the other nations. We should search for his law (words) and the written confirmation. Put your faith and hope on what is written down by the prophets of our God. When we do not speak or walk according to His words-(the written confirmation), we have no light of truth in us.

Mic 6:8. Our God has taught us what is good, and what is Yahuwah requiring from us? It is only to do what is right towards him and others. To love loyalty, and walk in modesty with our God. Do unto others as you want them to do to you is a right and good principle to live by. Our God is a loyal God to those who are loyal to him. Seeking and serving the gods of the other nations is showing disloyalty to our God- the only true God. That is a misstep our ancestors and us made in the past and should not make again. Doing the things our God commanded us to do is walking modestly with our God.

Isa 10:20. Our God foretold that in the final part of the day before He re-establish us again as His nation again, the remaining ones of Israel, survivors of the house of Jacob, would no longer support themselves or depend on the one who struck/enslaved them- (slave master). (We will no longer depend on the false teachings they have taught us about God in other to hold us in slavery to them). Rather we will support our self on Yahuwah our God, the holy one of Israel with faithfulness. Yes with all our heart, we will search and seek to know him through his written words and trust in him as our God to lead us into his will and decisions of long ago (Isa 26:8).

Prov 1:23, Heb 12:4-11. Accept his reproof or disciplining of us because of our ancestor's and our errors. Accept corrections in our hearts, seek to return and do right by our God. When we do, He promised to pour out his spirit on us and make his words known to us. The fact that you are still alive proves that your struggle with sins have not reached to the point where He will put all to death (Amos 9:10). So accept corrections today and return to your God before it is too late (Hos 6:1).

Act 2:21. Everyone who returns by calling on (seeking and praying to) the name of Yahuwah the God of Israel will be saved when time for His final judgment arrives (Isa 10:21-23. Ezek 20:36-38, Amos 9:10-12).

Mt 6:33, Isa 65:8-10. Keep on seeking first the kingdom of our God and his righteousness. What it is? What it will mean for those who are seeking that his holy name be free of all blame and sanctified in all the earth. What it will mean for his will to be done in all the earth?

Mic 5:8. The awakened remaining ones of Jacob have to be patience, endure until the end of the appointed time. Human hands will not remove your enemies- the occupiers of your Promised Land territory (Isa 8:7-9, 2Thess 1:6-10).

Isa 46:8-10, Ps 33:10-11. However, the decisions of our God still stand. He frustrates the schemes and plans of the nations. He will carry out his decisions and thoughts of his heart from generation to generation.

Few chosen ones by our God will inherit the promised blessings of Abraham.

John 6:44, 65. Unless you are chosen by our God, you cannot know God or come to Yahushua the leader of God's chosen people.

Mt 13:11-17. Since not all Israel are chosen, it is not granted to all to understand the sacred secrets of the kingdom of heaven. Mt 10:5-7. These kingdom secrets are mainly for the chosen ones to know. It is not for people of other nations but only for the lost sheep of house of Israel.

Why?

Amos 3:1-2, Gen 15:13-16. God is dealing with only the house of Israel, the descendants of Abraham with regards to the promise He made.

Hos 5:15, Hos 6:1-2, John 8:31-Isa 26:20. Not all but only the chosen one of Abraham's offspring- Jacobs are in punishment for their error until the anger /punishment time- (2000 years) ends.

How then are we to preach and teach or help them gain for themselves the salvation to come?

1pt 1:5, Isa 46:13. This salvation our God will grant to his chosen ones of Israel/Jacob in Zion at the last day. That is immediately after the 2000 years punishment imposed on them ends (Mt 24:29-31).

Gen 15:16-21, Isa 10:21-23. Salvation is therefore, the return of the 4th generation- the chosen ones of Abraham's chosen offspring back to the land/kingdom territory promised to them as an inheritance forever. Not all but the few chosen ones of Israel will return to Yahuwah the God of Israel to receive his mercy and salvation in Zion at the end of our punishment appointed time.

Lk 1:32-33, 69-75. Yahushua is the means to save the chosen ones of Israel and grant us salvation from all our enemies. He will then rule as king over the house of Jacob forever.

How should we preach?

John 4:22, Rom 9:4, Mt 10:11-15. Since salvation is first for the Hebrew Israelites- the Negroes; into whatever city or village you enter or go to. Search out who is deserving of the message- (lost sheep of house of Israel) and stay there until you leave. Mt10:5-7.

Why?

The message of the kingdom restoration time is not for all people, neither is it for all fleshly Israel. Therefore, some who are fleshly Israel will reject the message but the chosen ones will welcome it with joy and want to learn more. Our God will grant knowledge of himself and salvation to come to the chosen ones in the last day/appointed day (Hos 6:2-3).

Rom 9:1-13, 27-29. Paul was in grief and pain of heart because he wished that all his fleshly relatives who are Israelites... could be saved. However, it does not depend on him, but it all depends on God who calls or choses who will receive his salvation in the last day.

In like manner, today we do not know who our God will choose. We will like for all our relatives in the flesh who are Israelites, offspring of Abraham with regards to the promise to be saved.

John 6:44, 65, John 4:22, John8:32. However, it belongs to our God to choose who will obtain salvation in the last day.

Oppression and hatred will abound for the chosen ones.

Mt 10:16-20. The chosen ones will face opposition from men; they will be dragged to court... before kings and governors to testify of what is happening and coming upon the earth in the final days.

Why?

Ezek 39:7-23, Mt 24:29-30, Zeph 1:14-18. They will hear, see and know that God of Israel is the one distressing the nations to separate and gather back his chosen ones.

Mt 10:21-22, Mt 24:9, Lk 21:17, Mk13:13, Mt 10:34-39. Those not chosen will hate and hand over the chosen family members to be put to death. The chosen ones will be hated by all peoples on account of their God's name. That is on account of what He is doing –His vengeance on the nations. The chosen ones will be separated from those not chosen.

Since not all are chosen ones for salvation- our message

Mt 10:7, Zeph 1:14-18. Our message to the chosen ones is of encouragement for them to endure the distress upon humanity until it ends at its appointed time –year 2033. This distress being experienced in all nations is because our God- the kingdom of heaven has drawn near to take foretold actions to bring out from among the nations his chosen ones of Israel. The offspring of Abraham to inherit the Promised Land territory.

When?

Isa 43:1-7, Mt 24:29-31, Ps 119:105, Rev 2:10. Immediately after the 10 days = 10 years tribulation on the nations ends, the chosen ones of Israel will be gathered. This will be the hour/time of the final test for all the chosen ones.

Mt 10: 25-33, 2Pt 2:9, Acts 2:21. Not a single chosen one will fall to the ground without our father's notice and permission. Yahuwah knows how to deliver and protect his people out of distress. "Everyone who call on the name of Yahuwah will be saved".

Since not all are chosen- many will continue to lack knowledge of their God.

Deut 28:64, Ezek 20: 32, 39, Isa 8:11-17. Those not chosen will continue in their false worship and alliance with the nations/peoples.

Mt13:11-15, Hos 4:6, Amos 9:10. Those not chosen will continue in their ignorance or lack of knowledge of their God and will perish because of that lack of knowledge.

Mt 24:37:41. Those not chosen will pay no attention or understand that the end is upon them until it is too late as was in the days of Noah.

Israel, your salvation is not for keeping the laws, but because of our God's loyal love.

Deut 30:1-8. "When all these words come upon you, the blessing and the curse that I have put before you, and you call them to mind in all the nations where Yahuwah your God has dispersed you; 2 and you return to Yahuwah your God and listen to his voice according to all that I am commanding you today, you and your sons, with all your heart and all your soul; 3 Yahuwah your God will then bring back your captives and show you mercy and regather you from all the peoples where Yahuwah your God has scattered you. 4 Even if your people are dispersed to the extremity of the heavens, from there Yahuwah your God will gather you and bring you back. 5 Yahuwah your God will bring you into the land your fathers took possession of, and you will possess it; and he will make you prosper and will multiply you more than your fathers. 6 Yahuwah your God will cleanse your heart and the heart of your offspring, so that you will love Yahuwah your God with all your heart and all your soul and you may live. 7 Then

Yahuwah your God will bring all these curses upon your enemies, who hated and persecuted you. 8 "You will then return and listen to the voice of Yahuwah and observe all his commandments that I am commanding you today."

Why?

Deut 28:1-68. Our God foretold that Israel would first experience blessings for keeping His laws and commandment in the Promised Land. Israel will after experience the curses for not keeping the laws and commandment in the promise land. The curses for not keeping the laws in the land will follow Israel in all the places they are dispersed until the time for their awakening and remembering/recalling to mind all the things our God has foretold will happen to us (Isa 46:8-10).

Hos 5:15, Hos 6:1-2, 2Pt 3:8, Hos 3:4-5, Ezek 37:1-14, . This awakening and recalling to mind will occur in the final part of Israel's 2days = 2000 years punishment for our errors.

Yes, it is therefore, by faith in the promises of our God and his mercy will the chosen ones of Israel be saved.

Rom 3:21-24, Isa 14:1-3, John 6:44, 65. After a long time (2000 years) of abandoning Israel to bear punishment for their errors, Our God promised to show mercy to descendants of Jacob. He will return to save Israel when their power is waned (Deut 32:26-29, 36) because of His name that is involved with Israel, his inheritance.

Jer 31:34, 1John1:9, Isa 65:8-10. Our God will forgive all Israel who search for Him and beg for his mercy with resolve to return to Him and serve and obey him alone as God.

Jer 31:31-37, Lk 1:69-75, Isa 8:20. He will restore, establish a new covenant with his chosen ones of Israel and they will serve him in truth and faithfulness all their lives in the Promised Land.

Take the message continually to the lost sheep of house of Israel.

Amos 3:1. The lost sheep of house of Israel comprises of all the people of Israel that our God brought out of Egypt, who are now scattered and straying among all the nations bearing the punishment for their error until it ends.

Mt 10:6, Mt 15:24, Dan 9:25-26. The messiah –the leader, was sent to be the means to gather back the lost sheep of the house of Israel at the appointed time, after their scattering and straying (Deut 28:64, Ezek 36:5-16, Isa 53:6, Lk 1:69-75).

Why?

• Rom 9:4-5, Amos 3:1-2. To the lost sheep belong all the promises that God has made, including giving them his kingdom territory to possess as a lasting possession. God is only dealing with the offspring of Abraham with regards to the promise- Israel (Gen 15:13-21).

• Deut 7:5-6, 14:2, Exod 19:5, Mal 3:17. The lost sheep of Israel is a chosen nation and people to produce a special property for God. That is a kingdom of priests and kings to rule over the earth in righteousness Ps 135:4, Deut 26:18, Ps 45:16.

• Isa 65:8-10. From among the lost sheep of house of Israel, God will chose those who will inherit his mountain/kingdom. That is reason to take the message to the lost sheep of house of Israel and not to other nations and peoples.

Examples of Peter and Paul.

At Acts 3:26, 13:46. Peter and Paul first addressed the people of Judah with the message of salvation for the lost sheep of Israel. However, since many from Judah- (Jews) rejected the message, they will take it to the other Israelites scattered among the nations, those who will accept the invitation. Mt 22:1-14. Many are called but few will be chosen from among the lost sheep of house of Israel for the promised kingdom that will be established by their God. Isa 10:21-23, Amos 9:1-4, 8-12, Dan 2:44, 7:13-14, 27.

John 1:9-13, Acts 3:26, Acts 13:46. Like many from people of Judah in the 1st century. Many of the scattered sheep among the nations will not believe or put faith in the message of salvation for the house of Israel. To the few who will exercise faith, God will grant them authority to become his children. He will restore them to the kingdom He promised to their forefather-Abraham at the appointed time.

Babylon the great can no longer hold God's people captive by their false teachings.

Rev 18:4, Exo 28:64. She has fallen is the angels message to the chosen people of God. Her time of holding God's people captive has ended. "Get away from her mist if you do not want to share in her punishment that is coming.

John 4:22. The time is now; those chosen to worship Yahuwah our God, the God of Israel can now do so in truth and with spirit. Babylon the great can no longer dictate how we worship or lead us astray from our God (2Thess 2:3-12).

Why?

Prov 1:23, Joel 2:28-29, Acts 1:8, Eph 4:4. Our God will pour out his spirit in the last days on his chosen ones who accept His reproofing/discipline of us. He will then make his words known to us and we will no longer be carried captive by every wind of doctrine from wicked one-Babylon the great.

Isa 10:20, John 10:10. Then the chosen ones will no longer follow the teachings of the one (invaders) who struck and enslave our people. The spirit that we received in us will set us free from following other nations (John 8:32, 14:16-16, 26, Ezek 20:30-33).

Isa 61:1, Isa 11:2. That spirit is from our messiah and leader, the spirit of truth will break every yoke of slavery to the harlot- Babylon the great and set her captives free.

The spirit of truth.

1Cor 2:12, 1John 2:27. The spirit of truth from our God that we receive helps us to know the things given to us by our God so that we no longer follow the spirit of this world. That anointing spirit is now teaching you.

1John 2:20. That anointing taught the 1st century disciples of our God the true knowledge of our God and his activities. That same spirit is being poured out on us in these last days.

Why an all-powerful God allowed his chosen people to suffer, mistreated and be humiliated?

Gen 15:13, Jer 25:14, 11, Jer 29:10, 2Chron36:20, 21. Yahuwah foretold in advance that Abraham's chosen offspring will suffer through a series of mistreatment, exploitation and enslavement to other nations.

Examples.

Exod 1:8-14. The chosen descendants of Abraham were enslaved and mistreated in Egypt for 215 years.

2Chron 36:20-21. They were enslaved in Babylon for 70 years.

Joel 3:1-6. They were mistreated, exploited, and sold as slave to the Greeks.

Hos 5:15, 6:1-2, Mt 24:9, 19, 21-22. They will be mistreated and humiliated for 2days =2000yrs (great tribulation).

Deut 28:15-68. At present the chosen descendants of Abraham are still in their great tribulation, Scattered among the nations, sold as slaves, mistreated and brought lowest of all people.

Mt 7:20, Deut 28:64, 68. By their fruits, you will also recognize/identify the chosen people. E.g. The trans-Atlantic slave trade.

Why humiliated?

• Isa 46:8-10, Gen 15:13-16, Jer 25:14. Yahuwah foretold the outcome of what He wants to accomplish and how, to Abraham from the beginning. Abraham's chosen offspring will be mistreated and enslaved in land not theirs by many nations that God will judge to display his power at the end. Afterwards in their 4th generation/return to the Promised Land, they will possess the land forever.
Deut 32:25, 30-31, 36-43. God will judge all nations that mistreated and enslaved them and then return them to their land territory to possess it forever.

• Isa 45:5-7, 11-12. To prove his Godship to all. He allowed his sons, the works of his hands to go through afflictions and mistreatments before saving them for all to know that He is their God.
For Example. Rom 9:17 God allowed pharaoh to rise in power and mistreat and enslave Israel so that He can show his power over him and his nation. That way God's name will be declared in all the earth for the power God displayed.
Ezek 39:6-10, 21-29. Likewise, He allowed the nations to mistreat and enslave his chosen people so that at the end He will show his power over the

nations and have his name declared in all the earth as God of Israel.

• Acts 15:17-18, Amos 9:11-12, Isa 45:21. Yahuwah our God is the one who foretold and is doing all these things. He is the alpha and omega, author and finisher of our faith, the beginner and the end. His decisions of long ago will be carried out. He will save his chosen ones of Israel from their oppressors and enemies at the appointed time (Isa 46:13).

The suffering of the present time by the chosen ones of God cannot compare to their glory that will be revealed at the end.

Isa 46:13, Rom 8:18. God will grant salvation and his glory to Israel in Zion after their suffering time end.

The foretold sufferings.

Gen 15:13-16, Jer25:14. Abraham's offspring will experience many suffering, mistreatment and enslavement to other nations before they will be rescued and take possession of the land forever. Suffering started from Egypt to Babylon, Greeks, and Romans and until present time.

1Pt 5:9. The same foretold suffering is been experienced by all chosen offspring of Abraham with regards to the Promised Land until it ends.

Lk 21:24, Hos 6:1-2. At present the chosen offspring of Abraham is scattered among the nations bearing humiliation /great tribulation for 2days =2000yrs for their errors.

Lk 21:24, Isa 8:7-10, Mt 11:12. At present time, the promised kingdom /land territory for the chosen offspring of Abraham to inherit is taken over through violence means by other nations and peoples.

Mt 24:9, Mt 10:22, Deut 32:35. The chosen ones of Israel will be hated by all people on account of their God. They will be hated on account of the vengeance of their God coming on all flesh, peoples and nations. He is coming to save his chosen ones as He foretold long ago.

The glory to be revealed on the chosen ones of Abraham's offspring.

Gen 15:16. In the 4th generation of Abraham's offspring in the Promised Land, they will possess it forever. Ezek 36:1-12. Yes Israel was humiliated and their land taken over by others. However, a remnant of Israel from among the nations will return and inherit the land forever. They will be multiplied with many blessings as was before is the promise of our God.

Dan 2:44, Dan 7:12-14, 22, 27, Zech 8:1-8. God of Israel will setup his kingdom in Zion New Jerusalem. He will install his son as ruler over all. Ps 45:16-17. Sons of Israel will serve as co-rulers/princes in all the earth.

Rev 21:3-4, Zech 8:22-23, Zech 14:3,9, 11-18, Rev 22:1-5, Rev 21:10-27. God will dwell with his chosen ones of Israel in the Promised Land.

Amos 9:11-12, Ps 2:4-12. Israel will take possession of all other surviving nations and peoples and rule over them forever.

If a trumpet blows an unfamiliar tone, who will get ready for what is coming?

Amos 3:6-7, Ezek 33:4, 6. Yahuwah reveals what He is about to carry out to his chosen prophets of Israel who then warn the peoples by sounding the alarm.

Mt 20:1-13, Mt 4:17. The chosen ones -hired workers/watchmen knows at what time and what message to declare to the lost sheep of house of Israel at the appointed times of our God. Otherwise that worker is not sent and is a thief and of the lawless one. The faithful servants knows what time to blow the trumpet to alert/awaken God's people of the next appointed time or what is coming next in the scheduled calendar of the kingdom of heaven.

Timing pattern is important for the chosen ones to act and get the job done within the appointed time of our God. At 3.5yrs before the time of the next event, the messiah, our leader and the chosen disciples started to warn the people to repent because the time has drawn near for the kingdom of heaven to execute the next foretold event. We likewise will follow the same pattern to declare 3.5yrs before the next event-the gathering and return of Abraham's offspring to the Promised Land

and 3.5 years prior to the start of final ten years tribulation on the nations

Ps 32:8. Our God will give insight to the chosen ones and instruct us the way we should go, when and what time? He will give advice with his eye upon us.

Examples.

1st generation deliverance.
Exo12:1-31. Moses was told to tell the Israelites in Egypt of what to do and when/time to do it before their deliverance out of Egypt- (next event on the calendar of kingdom of heaven).

2nd generation deliverance and return.
2Chron 36:22-23, Isa 46:11, Isa 45:1-25. King Cyrus of Persia was the chosen one our God used to make the proclamation/ blow the trumpet signaling to the chosen people of Israel it is time to return to the Promised Land.

3rd generation deliverance and return.
Joel 3:2-6, Dan11:45. The kingdom of Greece took over the land from grand sea and holy mountain- Zion. They did abominable things until they came to their end. After the kingdom of Greece, remnants returned, fought and restore the temple and Jerusalem before the coming/birth of the messiah (Mal 3:1).

Mt 23:37-39, Lk 21:20-24. Yahushua our leader blew the trumpet to alert and gather the chosen few. He informed the chosen disciples of what is coming next, what will happen and when it will happen and what they are to do as the kingdom of heaven draw near to carry out the next foretold event-(Hos 5:15, Hos 6:1-2, Amos 9:1-4).

The 4th wild beast/kingdom –the Roman Empire arose to power in the world stage; the territory of Judea became subdued by Rome. The Roman government controlled the ruler ship in Jerusalem, Judea territory. Example is king Herod (a non-Israelite) appointed as ruler by the Cesar. Yes some Israelites were in the land but they do not have possession of the Promised Land for Abraham and his off springs. This led to the revolts against the Romans -invaders and oppressors (Isa 8:7-10) leading to the destruction and desolation of the nation as the messiah prophesied (Mt 24:2, Jer 25:14, Gen 15:13-16).

Deut 32:22-28, 35-36, Amos 9:1-10. Israelites were from then scattered among the nations, removed far away from their Promised Land by their God. They will not return to the land until after 2days =2000yrs punishment is ended and it is time for the 4th generation return to inherit the Promised Land to possess it forever.

The 4th generation deliverance and return.

Lk 1:69-75, John 10:9, 14, 16, Mt 15:24, 2Thess 1:6-10. Yahushua the messiah and leader is the mean of salvation and deliverance for the 4th generation of Abraham's off springs return to the Promised Land.

John 6:44, 65, Isa 65:8-10, Isa 46:13. The good news /trumpet about the appointed time for restoring and rebuilding the kingdom territory promised to Abraham's offspring will be declared by the chosen ones of Israel as the appointed time draws near for the kingdom of heaven to act.

Our God disciplines/trains everyone He chooses and receives as a son.

Heb 12:6, John 6:44. No one can come to truly know the father and the son unless the father choses and reveals himself to such one. Those chosen by him, He trains/disciplines for the responsibilities He will give to them.

Why?

Prov 13:24. Whoever holds back his rod of discipline hates his son, but the one who loves him disciplines/trains him diligently. Yahuwah loves his chosen ones of Israel; therefore He disciplines/trains them.

Discipline is training designed to produce a desired success in an assigned responsibility. God will not assign a responsibility without first training a person on how to handle the responsibility.

Example #1.

Yahushua our leader, messiah and chief agent of our faith.

Prov 8:22-31. He has years of observing, learning and training from the father to be the leader and savoir of sons of men. Heb 5:8, Heb 12:2-3. He was disciplined/ trained by our God. He endured shame, hostile speech from sinners and death on a torture stake.
Heb 2:10, Lk 17:25. The chief agent was perfected through sufferings for the role and responsibilities he will serve.

Example #2.

Israel's sons who will be adopted as sons of God to rule as princes in all the earth.
Ps 135:4, Isa 43:6-7, Gen 15:16, Isa 65:8-10, Ps 45:16-17. The chosen sons will inherit and possess the promised Land/kingdom of God forever and rule as princes in all the earth.

To assume that responsibility at the appointed time, Israel's sons need discipline/training and humiliation to fulfill their assigned responsibilities. Like their chief agent, the chosen ones will learn obedience through the things they suffered. That is through the trials and tribulation that came on Israel. Gen15:13, Jer 25:14, 1Pt 5:9.

Hos 6:1-2, lk 21:24. By the end of the discipline/suffering and punishment time of 2000 years, the chosen sons of Israel will have learned obedience. Mt 4:4, Lk 4:4, Heb 10:36, Heb 12:7-11.

Isa 61:3. They will have learned through their mourning/suffering over Zion.

Yahuwah, our God will let himself be searched for by those who have not asked for him...

Isa 65:1

Who are those who have not asked for and did not look for their God?

Deut 28:64, Hos 5:15, Mt 23:37-39, Lk 21:24, Zeph 1:6. Yahuwah foretold that He will scatter Israel among the nations, abandon them for a while. There they will be misled to forget about their God and serve other messiahs and gods of other nations (Mt24:4-5).

Hos 4:6, 1Jn 5:19, Hos 3:4-5. The misled people of Israel who have forgotten their origin-(who they are) and are now calling themselves by a different name given to them such as (African, African-American, Jamaican etc.) These who have forgotten who their God is, our God will let Himself be found by them, if they repent and turn around and seek for Him in the final parts of the days (2days=2000 years of their punishment).

Hos 6:1-2, 2Pt3:8. After 2days = 2000 years of being abandoned and punished without searching for and without knowledge of their God, the people of Israel scattered among the nations will return to seeking for Yahuwah their God and their true leader Yahushua-(David) their king in the final part of the days of their punishment time (Lk 1:32-33). Then He will let Himself be found by them.

Seek Yahuwah when He can be found.

Eccl 3:1, 6, Jer 29:13-14, Zeph 2:2-3. There is an appointed time for everything under the heaven, even a favorable time for people of Israel to search and seek to return to our God and be heard /found by Him.

Hos 6:1, Isa 26:20. It is not while people of Israel are serving punishment for their errors, but after or towards the end of their punishment is a favorable time to seek to return to our God.

Example

Dan 9:1-19. It is not while serving the 70yrs punishment in Babylon but towards the end of it did Prophet Daniel start to seek the face and search for the God of his ancestors. Seeking and pleading for Him to carry out the next foretold event concerning his people of Israel-(deliverance after 70 year in Babylon).

Hos 6:1-2, 2Pt 3:8. Likewise, not while serving the 2days = 2000yrs tribulation/ punishment are we to seek and be found by our God but towards the end, in the final part of the days. We are to earnestly seek for Yahuwah our God, seek for his mercy and forgiveness and restoration.

1260 days /3.5yrs before the end of punishment and final judgement of extermination –Isa 10:21-23 is a favorable time for those of Israel who have not searched for their God to return, seek to know Him before it is too late.

Yahuwah will reveal Himself In the appointed time to show favor to Israel.

Gen 15:16, Isa 49:8. When time of favor arrives for the return of the 4th generation of Abraham's offspring back to the Promised Land, our God will let Himself be found by his chosen ones of Israel to receive his mercy. He will answer and rescue us in his time of favor for us to inherit our desolated inheritances (Isa14:1-3, Ezek 36:1-12) in the final part of our 2000 years punishment.

Ezek 39:21-29, Isa 65:24. When that day come, our God will display his glory/power to save his people among the nations. They will see the judgment He has executed and power He will demonstrate among them. On that day, even before we call out to our God, He will answer, while we are speaking He will hear us because it is time to show favor to his inheritance, his chosen ones of Jacob.

Example

Mt 24:45-51. A person convicted and sentenced to serve time in prison will not be seeking favor/sympathy of the judge until he demonstrates that he has served the time given and have accepted correction for what he has done. Likewise people of Israel will not be shown favor/mercy until we have served the punishment time of 2000 years (Hos 6:1-2, 2Pt 3:8, Hos 3:4-5, Ps 84:10) for all our errors.

Isa 43:10, Isa 41:8, Mal 1:6, Isa 44:21. A wise slave/servant – (of Israel) will accept correction and be willing to do what the master required from him- (take care of the master's house hold as He directed/commanded).

Prov 1:23, 1Pt 5:6, James 4:10. These who accepted correction and are ready doing the right things while the master is away will be given the privilege of taking care of the master's household when He returns at appointed time (Hos5:15, Mt 25:50, Isa 8:17).

However, an unwise slave/servant of Israel will continue to be rebellious, saying that the master is delayed. He will start to beat up other slaves who are doing the right thing-(accept corrections). The wicked unwise slave of Israel, who is misled, will instead of accepting reproof will chose to go along with the drunkards and hypocrites of this world (Ps 2:1-12, Isa 8:9-12) who refuse to submit to the decision and will of our God. That unwise slave of Israel will receive the same judgment as the hypocrites and drunkards of this world (Amos 9:10-

12, Isa 10:21-23) when the master return at appointed time.

What will it profit a man if he gained the whole world and then lose his life?

Mk 8:36, Mt 16:26, Lk 9:25, Jam 4:13, Eccl 6:6. Our God initially did not allow for Israel to mingle with the nations/peoples because they are his special people to produce a special property (Deut 7:6, 14:2, Exo 19:5-6). However Israel kept choosing to gain the friendship of the world and therefore lost his life. Israel became dead as a nation because God gave Israel up to be humiliated for seeking friendship with the nations (Deut 32:16-30, Exek20:32, 39)

Who is the man?

Mt 7:16-20 "By their fruit you will know/recognize these men"- (Israel, Esau and the other nations).

How to gain the whole world

Be friends with everyone and try not to offend anyone. Let us all get along, each one do your own thing. E.g. be what you want to be. LGBT, murderers, idolaters, Satan worshipers, hypocrites, love one another, we all serve the same God, God created all of us. You are not the judge of me.

Mt 24:48-51. The evil unwise slave of Israel will start to beat up his fellow slaves who are trying to do the right thing – (accept correction and return to their God commands) (Isa 8:10-15).

The unwise slave/servant of Israel will chose to gain the friendship of the world and go on partying with the hypocrites and drunkards of this world. He joins them in their rebellious ways (Ps 2:1-12).

James 4:4, Mk 8:38. Friendship with the world is enmity with our God. Choosing to hide the truth of his words in this adulterous and sinful generation is choosing the friendship of the world over the God of Israel. That means gaining the world as a friend but losing your soul/life in exchange in the end. (Amos 9:10-12, Ezek 32-39).

All Israel went astray trying to gain the friendship of the world.

Ezek 20:32, 39, Isa53:6, Rom3:23, 6:23, Ps84:10. All Israel wandered away, we are to stay 2days =2000yrs in the tent of wickedness. For this all Israel has sinned and fallen short of the glory of God. The wages or judgment on all Israel is then death (Isa 10:21-23, Amos 9:10-12).

Isa 14:1-3, Rom 3:24-25, Rom 9:15-18. However, due to the mercy or kindness of our God, many Israelites will be declared righteous due to the release by ransom paid by Yahushua, the messiah.

Salvation for Israelites who repent and turnaround from following after the nations.

Deut 30:1-8, John 4:22. Our God will show mercy and restore his people of Israel who repent and seek to return to him in the final days of their punishment/tribulation time.
Gen15:16, Isa 65:8-10, Mt 24:29-31. He will restore them to the land He promised to Abraham and his offspring to inherit forever.

Are we now in the final part of the days yet?

Hos 6:1-2. Israel will receive punishment from their God for 2days then restored on the 3rd day.

It depends on which days you are referencing. Is it the final days of punishment and tribulation on Israel or the final days before the restoration of Zion?

Days of punishment and vengeance of God on Israel.

Deut 32:15-28, 35-36. It was foretold.

Hos 5:15, Hos 6:1-2. Details of how it will be done.

Mt 23:37-39, Lk 21:20-24. Starting point of execution of God's vengeance on Israel is the year AD 33.

Hos 6:1-2, 2Pt 3:8. Duration of God's vengeance on Israel is 2days =2000yrs.

Length = AD 33 + 2000yrs = year 2033

Last days / remaining days of punishment /vengeance appointed time.

Year 2033 – present day (2019) =14yrs more.

Isa 26:20, MT 24:13, Mt 10:22. The chosen ones of Israel should endure until the end of God's wrath / punishment time on Israel is passed/over.

Isa 66:15-16, Jer 25:29-35, Rev 2:10. Towards the end of the punishment on all Israel, a ten days = 10 years tribulation and of Judgment on all flesh will begin.

Isa 10:21-23, Isa 65:15, Amos 9:1-4, 10-12, Ezek 20:34-38. The extermination of unrepentant rebels of Israel will take place during this period.

Deut 32:31-35, 37-43, Joel 3:2-21, Zeph 1:14-18, Zeph 2:3-15, 3:8. Judgment day of the other nations and peoples will also take place during this final ten years from 2023- 2033.

Which God /gods do you call upon?

The only true God who is He?
John 17:3, 1John5:20, Isa 46:3-13, Deut 32:15, Deut 33:26

He is the God of Israel.
Isa 45:3-7. The one doing all things.
Ps 83:18. Yahuwah is his name.

Ezek 39:7-8, 21-29. He will make his holy name known among his people of Israel; to prove that He is their God alone. He will restore the captives of Jacob and have mercy on the whole house of Israel.

Deut 32:9, Jer 25:14. As for other nations and peoples, the true God will judge them for what they have done to his inheritance – Israel. Joel 3:2-21, mic 1:3-5, Isa 8:8-10, Deut 32:41-43.

Ps 147:19-20, Amos 3:1-2, Isa 46:10. The true God reveals his laws and judgment to Jacob/Israel his people but not to any other nations /peoples. They know nothing about his judgments and decisions that are coming.

The gods of the other nations and peoples.

Deut 32:31-34. Their rock or god is not like the true God -our God, the God of Israel. Their gods cannot compared to or be likened to Yahuwah the true God. Isa 46:5-6, Isa 40:19, Jer 10:8, 9.

The works of human hand

Gen 27:40, Isa 44:16-17, Dan 3:1, 5. Their gods are the works of their hands that they trust in; such as weapons, guns, bullets, bombs (weapons of mass destructions).
Jer 10:9, Jer 51:17. Their gods are idols made with human hands such as the sword/cross, image made by a craftsman.

False gods

Deut 28:64, Mt 24:4-5, Rom 1:24-25. What the nations call gods or messiahs are false and imitations made to deceive and mislead people. For example, god, lord, Jesus Christ etc. are all false invented imitations of the true God of Israel and the messiah of Israel. These false gods and false messiahs are raised up to mislead and provide false hope to even the misled people of Israel. Examples of false hope are "all people go to heaven after death" or "the kingdom of God is for everyone to inherit" or "the earth will become a paradise"

Our God will carry out his decisions and counsels despite the oppositions from the nations /peoples.

Isa 46:8-10. His decisions and his will still stands and will be carried out at appointed times.

Amos 3:1-2, 7, Mt 26:54, Mk 12:24. The decisions/things He revealed through his prophets of Israel will be fulfilled as it is written in the scriptures.

Isa 46:11, Isa 45:25, Isa 45:5-7. God has the power to make his decisions, will and prophesy of his prophets to be fulfilled.

God's decisions regarding the earth.

Isa 45:18, Rev 11:18. He formed the earth to be inhabited and not to be destroyed by man. Therefore He will take action to set matters straight, restore and heal the earth. He will bring to ruin those ruining the earth.
Mic 1:3-5. Earth's high places will be treaded down to start all over.
Mt 24:37-41. As it was in the days of Noah so it will be in the day of the son of man.

2Pt 2:5-12, 2Pt 3:5-8. Heaven and earth that are now are stored up for fire- until the day for destruction of ungodly men- (those not of God who oppose his will and decisions).

God's decisions regarding his people of Israel.

Amos 9:1-4, 10, Amos 3:1-2. After the messiah the leader and chief corner stone is stroked and put to death, the forewarned calamity will follow the people of Israel until the sinners are annihilated.

Hos 5:15, Hos 6:1-2, Hos 3:4-5. God will then go away and return to his place in heaven. Israel will bear punishment for their errors for 2days /2000 years (2Pt 3:8).

Lk 21:24. People of Israel will be lead away as captive into all the nations to serve the punishment until it ends after 2000 years. The Promised Land to Israel /Jerusalem will be trampled by the gentile nations until the appointed time given to them is over.

Ezek 20:36-38, Amos 9:11-12, Ezek 36:6-12. After Israel have served their 2000 years punishment among the nations- (outside of the Promised Land), God will return to bring them out from among these nations back to the land he promised Abraham and his offspring to possess in their 4th generation as a lasting inheritance (Gen15:16).

Jer 25:14, Deut 32: 37-43, Ezek 39:7, 21-29. Our God will display his power among the nations and execute judgment on the nations before restoring the captives of Jacob/Israel to their promised land to inherit it forever.

Dan 2:44, Dan 7:13-14, 21-22, Lk 1:32-33, 69-75. Our God will setup his kingdom with his repurchased ones of Israel. His son will be enthroned as king in Zion to rule over Israel and the remaining ones of the nations.

God's decisions regarding other nations and peoples.

Deut 32:31-34, 37-43. He will render vengeance on all other nations and peoples for what they have done to Israel his people and their land.
Joel 3:2-21, Zech.14:3-15. The nations/peoples should prepare for war with our God – the God of Israel because it is coming after Israel's punishment ends. The scriptures must be fulfilled.

Ps 2:1-12, Zech 8:1-8, 20-23, Zech 14:16-21. The remaining nations/peoples after the war will kiss/honor and submit their authority to the son of God-(Yahushua) enthroned as ruler over Zion or perish in the way. Only the chosen people of Israel will have the privilege of rendering sacred service to Yahuwah our God in the house of our God (Lk 1:69-75, Rom 9:4).

The hour of the final test

Rev 3:10. The hour of a final test to come upon the inhabitants of the earth.

Test about what?

Isa 10:20-23, Ezek 20:34-38, Amos 9:10-15. For the Israelites, it is a test to determine who will be salvaged to return to the kingdom territory and who will be exterminated. It will be a test to determine who is in mourning over Zion and who prefer to join as one with the nations to serve their false gods under one world government.

Hos 6:1-2, 2Pt 3:8, Rev 2:10. This final test will start in the last 10 years of the 2000 years punishment and correction time on all Israel.
Isa 65:8-10. It will be very difficult to pass a chemistry test if you have never taken a chemistry course at school. Likewise, it will be very difficult to pass this hour of the final test if an Israelite has not taken time to seek, search and take in knowledge of their God and his activities of what is coming.

Deut 28:64, Isa 8:10-14. Do not be misled to continue to follow the invaders nations- (Assyrian, Babylon, Greece and Romans) that came against Israel to keep worshiping other gods.

Ezek 20:32, 39. The time allowed by our God for all Israel to go and serve the gods of other nations will have been over by the time of this final test.

Seek life, not death.

John 17:3, Hos 4:6. By taking in and acquiring accurate knowledge of the only true God and the son He sent, it will mean life for those who knew how. But lack of true knowledge of our God will result in death.

Acts 2:21, Joel 2:32, Rom 10:13. Everyone who calls on the name of Yahuwah, the God of Israel will be saved/ preserved alive during the hour of the final test.

Isa 46:13, Zech 8:20-23, Amos 9:11-12. Every one of the other nations/peoples who will abandon their false gods and lies and are willing to join the people of Israel to seek the favor of the true God of Israel will be preserved alive.

Basis of the final test.

John 1:9-12, John 3:18, John 8:1. God sent his Son into the world, that those who accept him as their ruler and king will not be destroyed but will be preserved in the hour of the final test.

Ps 2:6-12. Will the nations and peoples accept and submit to the ruling authority of the son of God to be enthroned in Zion or will they rebel? Their choice will determine their fate after the final ten years prior to 2033.

The first test was out of Egypt.

Deut 8:1-4. He put our forefathers to the test to know what was in their hearts. To know if they will keep his commandments or not. He humbled them and let Israel go hungry ...for 40yrs in the wilderness.

Mt 4:4, Lk 4:4. The lesson is to humble them and teach them that man must live not on bread and meat alone but also by observing every word and commandments from our God must we live by. Many of our ancestors failed in the first test.

The final hour of the test will be out from among the nations.

Deut 28:64, Lk 21:24, Ezek 20:34-38. People of Israel were scattered among the nations for our failing to retain the lesson of the first test. Therefore a final hour test is coming to determine who will live or who will be exterminated (Isa 10:21-23, Amos 9:10-12). Who has learned the lesson and who has not?

Ps 84:10, Ps 26:8, Ps27:4, Hos 5:15, Hos 6:1-2, 2Pt 3:8. The lesson of the final hour test will be to experience the difference between living under the tent and protection of our God and living without it in the tent of wickedness. In the end, we can either chose to accept his ruling over us through his son or as rebels reject it and perish in the way (Ezek 20:33, Ps 2:1-12).

Everyone who calls on the name of Yahuwah the God of Israel will be saved

Act 2:21, Rom 10:13-16. In the final part of the days-(days of Israel serving punishment for our errors), everyone who calls on the name of Yahuwah (seeks the favor of God of Israel) will be saved.

John 4:22, Zech 8:20-23, Rom 9:16-18. Both people of Israel and other nations can be saved, however, there are those who He reserved to receive his wrath (Isa 10:21-23, Amos 9:10-12).

Deut 28:64, Isa 46:13, Ezek 20:39. Both people of Israel and other nations/peoples will first leave their worship of false gods and their false teachings to earnestly seek the God of Israel.

Ps 147:19-20, Zech 8:20, Ezek 7:21-22, Ezek 23:39, Ezek 36:21-23, Ezek 39:7. Other nations/peoples will have to abandon their profaning of the true God's name by their teaching and trying to serve as his spokesman/ministers. They are not his chosen to do that, the chosen ones of Israel are his chosen ones to serve as ministers of our God (Deut 7:6, 14:2, Zech 14:16-21, Rom 9:4, Lk 1:69-75).

Ps 45:16. The chosen ones of Israel are to serve as a special property – (kings and priests/rulers and ministers) of our God in all the earth.

Ps 2:1-12. Other nations and people can be loyal subjects of the kingdom or ruler ship in Zion if they fear the God of Israel and honor the son enthroned as king in Zion. If they rebel, they will perish in the way.

How?

It is not by simply saying or mentioning a specific name such as Jesus, Lord, God, Yahweh, Yahuwah, etc. but it is by knowing and declaring the authority and powers behind the God of Israel and trusting in and worshiping Him can everyone be saved. Everyone who trusts in the name, authority, and power of Yahuwah the God of Israel and follows his instructions and commandments as revealed in his words will be saved.

I will declare and call on the name of Yahuwah- our God

Deut 32:3. "I will declare the name of Yahuwah. Tell about the greatness of our God!" Moses declared the name of God by telling all Israel of the qualities belonging to the only true God. The God that has chosen Israel to be his people.

How did Moses declare the name of our God?

Deut 32:3-4. By telling of the greatness and Excellency of our God above all other gods.
• He told of His being perfect in all His decisions, activities and actions.
• He told of his ways as the ways of justice.
• He told of His being a God of faithfulness who is never unjust.
• He told of His showing of loyal love up to a thousand generations to those who love him.
• He told of His being a righteous and upright God.
• He told of His being a God of vengeance to his enemies (those who hate Him)

Yahushua (Jesus) declared or made his name known.

John 17:26. Making his name known involves telling of his wonderful qualities such as his great power, wisdom, mightiness, faithfulness, great justice, foreknowledge, mercy, etc. It includes all characteristics associated with the name, even his great vengeance (Heb10:31).

So will you declare the name of our God?

Deut 10:17. Who is the God above all other gods? Yahuwah!

Ps 147:5. Who is the God mighty in power? Yahuwah!

Isa 45:5-6. Who has no one his equal? Yahuwah!

Dan 2:20. Who is the all-wise God? Yahuwah!

Isa 30:18. Who is the God of great justice? Yahuwah!

Jer 9:24. Who is the most loyal, and shows loyal love? Yahuwah!

Isa 14:1. Who is the God to show mercy to Jacob? Yahuwah!

Jer 31:11. Who is the God that will redeem Israel? Yahuwah!

Deut 7:9. Who is the God, faithful to all His promises? Yahuwah!

Isa 46:10. Who is the God that can tell the future from the beginning Yahuwah!

Deut 32:35. Who is the God that will take vengeance for his people? Yahuwah!

Act 10:34. Who is the God that shows no partiality but favors? Yahuwah!

We declare our God's name by telling of the wonderful things He has done and will do for His

Chosen people –Israel and everyone who submit to his decisions and ruling (Ps2:10-12).

56

The people of Israel will dwell for a long time without a king or a prince...

Hos 3:4-5

When will Israel dwell without a king or a prince?

Gen 49:10, Dan 9:25-26. The staff of ruler ship will not depart from Judah/Judea/Israel until Shiloh (last king of Israel) arrives/appears. After that, Israel will dwell without a king or a prince to rule over and shepherd them for a long time.

Who was the last king of Judea/Israel?

Mt 2:2, Mt27:11, 29, John 18:39, John 19:3, 19-22. Yahushua is the last king of the Judah/Israel.

He died a horrible and shameful death for the sins of his people. He was crowned in shame and humiliation, however, He will return with power and great glory at the appointed time.

From his death until now-year 2019 A.D, the people of Israel has dwelt for a long time without a king or a prince from Israel to gather them and shepherd them.

Hos 6:1-2, 2Pt3:8, Isa 46:9-10. For 2days/2000yrs the people of Israel will dwell without a king or a prince to lead them until it ends.

Mt 24:29-31. However, Immediately after Israel's 2000yrs tribulation ends, the sign of our king and messiah returning will appear in heaven. He will return with his angel to gather back his chosen ones of Israel back to their promised land.

Lk1:32-33, 69-75. He will rule as king over the house of Jacob forever.

Dwell a long time without a sacrifice?

Heb 3:1, Heb 4:15, Heb 7:26, Heb 9:11, 25. The last sacrifice made on behalf of the people of Israel is the one made by their last king of Israel and high priest. Since then there is no other sacrifice to be made on behalf of the sins of the people of Israel. Whoever of Israel that puts faith in that last sacrifice and approach God based on the blood of the one sacrificed-(Yahushua) will have their sins forgiven by our God. For there is no salvation in any other name.

Dwell for a long time without a pillar /a homeland.

Hos 6:1-2, Lk 21:24, Lam 1:7-21. For 2000yrs the people of Israel will be in tribulation/punishment for sins. They will have no homeland of their own during this period. They will be scattered among the nations to serve punishment for their errors. Their Promised Land inheritance will be taken over by the gentile nations and trampled until the appointed time is fulfilled.

Dwell for a long time without an ephod?

For a long time, the people of Israel will dwell without an ephod– a means – (the Holy Spirit) to discern the will of God for the people of Israel to know. Israel will dwell a long time without one who serves as servants or prophets having the spirit (ephod cloth on them) to discern and tell the people the will of our God.

The ephod linen is a symbol of having the spirit of God on an individual. However, in the final part of the days, including the 2days/ 2000yrs of punishment on people of Israel; our God promised to pour out His holy spirit on all sorts of flesh- people of Israel. Joel 2:28-29, Ezek 39:29.

John 14:15-20, 26, Isa 8:10-12. After a long time of dwelling without an ephod, following other nation's decisions, plans and conspiracy, our king will ask the Father and He will give to us the helper –Holy Spirit of truth that He promised. That Holy Spirit will be with us forever and teach and bring back to our minds the things our messiah and our God taught us. These things are written for our comfort and endurance (Rom 15:4). However, we must read and study his words to receive the help of the Holy Spirit.

Pro 1:23, Isa 10:20. Once we accept his 2000 years reproofing of us and turnaround from following the nations, our God will pour out his spirit on us and make his written words known to us.

Dwell for a long without a teraphim statues?

Hos 5:15, Hos 6:1-2, 2Pt 3:8, Deut 28:64, Isa 46:9-10. Our God foretold that He will abandon his people Israel and return to his place in heaven. Israel will bear the punishment for 2000 years for our errors. During this appointed time, Israel will have no teraphim statues-(God of their own) rather Israel will be misled to worship and serve gods of other nations (such as Zeus, Jesus Christ, Baal, lord, god, etc.).

God has planned the salvation of Israel- his people from the founding of the world.

Gen 15:13-16, Mt 25:34, Rev 17:8. The world /nation of Israel was founded by Yahuwah when He called out Abraham to obey Him. God told Abraham of the calamities that will happen to his descendant. He made the promise to grant salvation to Abraham's chosen descendant in their 4th generation in the Promised Land. Then Abraham's offspring-Israel will possess the land promised forever. From the founding of the world, God has it written down that the chosen seed of Abraham will take possession of the kingdom territory He promised to Abraham.

Deut 31:16-21, 27-29, Deut 32:5-35-43. Even before delivered Israelites out of Egypt were to take possession of the Promised Land for the 1st generation, God foretold what will befall them in the land that they are crossing over to take as a possession. The scriptures must be fulfilled as foretold.

Isa 63:17-19. Israel possessed the Promised Land for a short time, then their enemies-(Amorites) took over and trampled the land. Israel was taken out of the land for 70yrs to Babylon to serve punishment for their rebellion.

Dan 9:1-3. After 70yrs is passed, Abraham's offspring –Israel returned to the Promised Land for the 2nd generation of Abraham's offspring to possess the Promised Land.

Isa 26:18, Isa 63:17-19, Dan 8:21-22, Joel 3:2-6. Israel rebuilds and possessed the Promised Land for another short time and then it was taken out of it by the enemies. This time the kingdom of Greeks took possession of the land from the great sea to the holy mountain until it was taken out of the way by the Romans.

The Maccabees took possession of the land, rebuild and restore it for a short time – (3rd generation return) before Rome took over possession of the land.

Mt 24:2, John 19:19, 23. In AD 33 The Roman ruler and soldiers put to death the Last-king of the Jews/Israel. In 70 AD the Roman soldiers destroyed the nation to the ground and the remaining Israelites where scattered among the nation until the time for the 4th generation return to the Promised Land.

Isa 46:13, Mt24:29-31, Zech 8:1-8, Mt25:34. God will grant the salvation He foretold for Abraham's offspring in the Promised Land.

Hos 6:1-2, 2Pt 3:8, 2Thes 1:6-10. This salvation will occur immediately after the 2000 years tribulation /punishment on all Israel ends.

Our God sends out his messengers ahead before His visiting of his people and the earth for judgment.

Gen 6:13-20, Isa 40:3, Mal 3:1, and Lk 1:10-11

Why?

• Gen 6:17, Exod 3:16-17, Lk 1:13, Mt 24:2, Lk 21:22-24. To inform His chosen people of his favor/mercy and of the appointed time event that is coming next.
• Gen 6:18-22, Exod 3:18-22, Lk 1:15, Lk21:20-21. To pass instructions of what the chosen ones have to do to avoid the calamitous judgment that is coming.
• Gen 6:18, Exod 8:22-22, LK 1:17, Mt 10:34-36, Mt 24:31, 40-41. To create a division or separation between those fearing him and the wicked, rebellious people. A separation between those who like the wicked ways things are going and those who want to return to God's rules. A division between those who choose to worship the wild beasts out of the seas and those who want to return to God's decision and will (Isa 46:9-10, Ps 2:1-12).

Who are God's messengers/ message carriers?

• The angels of God. Those sent to declare and carry out His will- the next appointed time /event of our

God. Lk 1:11-17, 19, Mt 25:31, 2Thess 1:7, Ps 103:20, Isa 37:36.

• Human messengers or message carriers – (His prophets of Israel) He reveals His words and next appointed time event to only his prophets of Israel. Ps 147:19-20, Amos 3:1-2, 7, Isa43:10, Isa 41:8, Isa 42:9, Dan 9:22, Rev 1:1.

Purpose of the messenger.

• Deliver God's messages to the Human messengers/message carriers-(of Israel). Lk 1:17
• Deliver God's instructions of actions that must be carried out.
• Lead those in expectation of our God to carry out His instructions at the appointed time. Isa 8:17-20, 2Chron 20:17-22

Test every messenger or message carrier whether they are of God.

1Jn 4:1, Mt24:4-5, 24, Lk 1:18-20. "...test every inspired statement, for many false prophets have gone into the world misleading and exploiting the people. Zechariah tested the angle that was sent to him.

Example. If a messenger/prophet speaks and declares that the world will end tomorrow or next year. Test that statement: what is proof or evidence supporting the statement? Is the statement supported by the written and revealed words of the God of Israel?

Deut 18:20-21. If it is not based on the evidence of the written words of our God. Do not put trust in that prophet/messenger.

Ps 78:41, 1Corr 10:9. Test the messenger not in terms of resisting the holy one of Israel, but as in seeking supporting evidence for the statement. A testimonial evident of 2 or 3 has no challenge.

Lk 1:19-20. Seek evident supporting and leading to the fulfillment of the statement.

The chosen ones will leave everything to seek to return to the kingdom.

Jn 6:44, Mt 19:27, Mk 10:28, Lk18:28. "We have left everything to follow you," Peter said. Yes for 3.5 yrs. The chosen ones left everything to follow the messiah in declaring the good news that the kingdom of heaven has drawn near to execute the next appointed event to come. In a like pattern, the chosen ones will declare the good news about the kingdom of heaven drawing near to restore the earthly kingdom (footstool of our God).

Mt 10:5-21, Lk 1:16-17. They will start to prophesy/declare the good news 3.5 years before the kingdom restoration appointed time in compliance with the master's instructions. They will prophesy and get ready for our God a prepared people /sheep to return back to the pen/kingdom of their father and God.

The chosen ones for this work will leave everything (mother, father, sons, and daughters who do not put faith in the good news of kingdom restoration drawing near) to follow the footsteps of the messiah.

*Why leave everything to seek first the return to
the kingdom?*

• Mt10:22-24, Ezek 20:39-44, Hos 6:1-2. It is a test of where your heart and love is. Do you love your God to the point of leaving the world and its attractions (glory of Egypt) behind to seek to return and serve him alone in his kingdom?
• John 14:1-3. Our leader and king have gone to prepare dwelling places (houses) etc. in the kingdom for those who are his. Enough houses for everyone who will follow his footsteps.
• Eccl 5:16, Lk12:15-40. What benefit is there for a person to seek to safeguard his soul by gaining the whole world but then lost his life anyway. It is better to store up treasures in heaven with our God than here on earth where the winds of destruction will carry them away.
• Isa10:21-23, Lk 12:32, Isa 65:8-10. Only a little flock out of the chosen people of Israel will leave everything to seek to return to the kingdom. The chosen ones, the little flock that the father has agreed to give the kingdom.
• Mt 6:33, Jer 31:21. Those who researched and acquired an accurate knowledge of the kingdom, who set up signposts/road markers as to when is the time for the return to occur, will be willing to leave everything to seek to return to the kingdom.

Mt 5:3, Mt 6:9-10. The kingdom of God is for those conscious of their spiritual need for God. Those who desire God's rule over their lives.

Dan 2:44, Gen 15:16. God will set up his kingdom in the 4th generation of Abraham's offspring in the kingdom territory.

Jn 18:36, Lk 21:24. The kingdom will be established at the right time after the gentile times (of this world) ends.

Mt 11:12, Lk 21:24. The kingdom territory will continue to be under violent at the hand of the gentile nations until their time ends, while Israel is scattered among the nations to serve punishment for their errors.

Hos 6:1-2, 2Pt 3:8, Isa 26:20. Punishment and tribulation on Israel will last for 2days/2000 years before the chosen ones of Israel will return back to the kingdom territory to possess it forever.

Lk 21:31. Those watching and observing the signs will discern when to leave everything and seek to be restored to the kingdom. They will leave the ways of life of the nations to declare the good news of the

next event of the kingdom of heaven (Mt 6:32, 2Pt
3:11).

The chosen race/ people- Israel is under tribulation/punishment in the world.

Deut 7:6, Deut 14:2, John 16:33, Lk 21:24, Mt 24:21, Jn 17:11. Negro-Israel is the chosen people to serve the true God. But because of error, Negro-Israel is scattered among the nations to serve punishment for their errors.

Hos 5:15, Hos 6:1-2, 2Pt 3:8. Negro-Israel will be in tribulation /punishment until they complete the punishment time of 2days=2000yrs. This will be a great tribulation/punishment such as has never occurred on any nation under heaven.

Signs of the great tribulation on Israel.

Hos 3:4-5, Lk 21:24, Mt 24:2. For a long time, the people of Israel will dwell without a pillar or an Identifiable homeland of their own. Their homeland will be taken over by other invader nations by violent means (Mt 11:12).

Gen 15:13, Deut 28:48, 64, Jer 25:14, Isa 26:13. Israel will be a slave/servant to many nations around them during this great tribulation. They will slave to build and develop other nations/people's land but not their own land- (The Promised Land to Abraham by God- Gen 15:13-21).

Deut 32:23-25, Amos 9:1-5. The people of Israel will face many hardships among these nations. They will be in hunger and thirsty, in wants or lacks of means, in wars and sickness. They will rise up as a people and then fall low because of the curses (Deut 28:15-68).

Isa 63:19, Hos 5:15, Mt 23:37-39. Because of the tribulation, people of Israel became like a people whom God has never ruled over-(strangers to their God). They were abandoned for a long time to the wild beasts to tear to pieces.
Deut 28:65-68, Isa 9:16, Isa 63:17, Isa 3:12. The people of Israel all have the confusion of hearts because of not knowing what will be coming next or what to do next because of the great tribulation. For example, Should we stay in America or should we move/ flee to Africa? Should we stay as one Nigeria or should we break away and be on our own because of oppression.

Deut 28:68, Jer25:14. The descendants of Israel were captured and taken into slavery (Egypt) again by ships to identify them with the great tribulation on the people.
Amos 9:7, Isa 26:20, Mt 7:21, Hos 5:15. God can identify his chosen people who are in great tribulation/ punishment scattered among the

nations doing His will. They look like the sons of Ethiopia/ Cushite.

The scriptures must be fulfilled.

Mt 24:21, Mk 13:19. The 2000 years great tribulation on the people of Israel will not occur again after it ends.

Mt 24:9. Israel was handed over to the great tribulation caused by their enemies. Israel as a nation became dead/killed, hated by all nations on account of their God's name. It is no wonder the people who caused tribulation on Israel have no human conscience as seen in the atrocities they inflicted on the people of Negro-Israel.

Rom 12:12, John 16:33, Heb 11:37, 2Cor 4:17, Rev 2:10. The 2days = 2000 years great tribulation on Israel is not permanent but temporary (Hos 6:1-2, 2Pt 3:8). Chosen people of Israel have to endure the tribulation until it ends. Learn endurance from it.

Rom 8:35, Amos 3:1-2. Not even this great tribulation will be able to separate the chosen people –Israel from the love of our God and our king and leader- Yahushua.

Rev 2:10. Israel, your enemy/enemies that caused and is causing your tribulation until it ends is known as the devil.

2Thess 1:6-10, Rom 2:9, Deut 32:36-43, Deut 30:7. Our God will repay tribulation to those who have caused tribulation on his people of Israel when He returns from heaven with his angels.

Rev 2:9, 3:9, Joel 3:2-6. Those who now claim that they are the chosen people of God but are not; but have taken over the land and inheritance belonging to the true chosen people of Israel will receive the vengeance of our God at his presence.

Rev 12:9. These ones are of the devil deceiving the entire inhabited earth with their lies that they are the chosen people of Israel.

Mk 13:24, Mt 24:29-31, 2Thess 1:6-8, Gen 15:16. Immediately after the 2000 years tribulation/punishment on all Israel ends, our leader and king will return from heaven to make war and gather back his chosen ones to the land/ kingdom promised to Abraham and his offspring to possess forever.

Lk 1:32-33, 69-75, 2Thess 1:7, Rom 9:4. People of Israel will then be given relief from all their tribulations. They will then render sacred service to their God and king.

Proof that the Negro-Israel are serving gods of other nations

Deut 28:64. God will scatter Israel among the nations and there they will serve gods of other nations.

• Gen 15:13-21. You/we are living in a land not ours/your own. We are not in the land promised to Abraham and his offspring to inherit forever in the 4th generation. The land territory Israel will inherit, build up and establish as the kingdom of God of Israel. We are building and developing lands that are not ours such as America, islands, Brazil, Africa, Japan, Russia, etc. and all the places we were scattered.
• Your taxes, contributions, and sacrifices where does it go? Which nation is it being used to build? Which god is it being used to exalt? Examples.
Catholic Church contributions go to Rome-Vatican and exalt Roman Christianity god and build up Rome. Church of England's contributions goes to England; it builds up England and exalts their god. American churches-(Scientology, Mormon, JW, Baptist, etc.) Contributions go to America and help builds up America and their Christianity god. Russian Orthodox Church contributions go to Russia and help build and exalt the god of Russia.

The God of Israel and the contributions of his people.

Contributions of the people of Israel should go to Zion, Jerusalem to help exalt the God of Israel. However, the people of Israel have no pillar-(homeland of their own) (Hos 3:4-5, Hos 5:15).
• Zech 8:1-8. If the headquarter of the organization you belong to is in any other place but Zion, then you are worshipping and serving gods of other nations and building up other nations with your contributions.
• Ezek 20:39-42. God of Israel will bring out his people from among the nations back to His holy mountain Zion to serve him alone. He will require their contributions then.
• Ezek 20:32, 39, Ezek 37:1-14. All Israel went to serve the gods of other nations. However, our God is now awakening us that we should return and serve him alone.
• Ezek 20:40-44, Hos 6:1. We should return and feel ashamed for our conduct-(leaving the true God to go and serve false gods of the nations.
• Eph1:8, Hos 6:1-2, Deut 30:1-10. Now that you are enlightened, will you turn around or will you continue to serve the gods of other nations (Heb 6:4-6).

Yahuwah your God will cleanse you.

Ezek 36:25, Mal 3:3, Deut 30:6, Ezek 36:33. The chosen ones of Israel will be cleansed and purified by our God of their contaminations from the nations. Cleansed from idolatry worshipping of false gods, cleansed from being misled by false Christs, messiahs, and leaders. Cleansed from the wicked, immoral conducts of the nations. Cleansed to sanctify the Sabbaths in the Promised Land.

Why?

Deut 28:64, Ezek 20:30-32, 39. When people of Israel were scattered among the nations for 2000 years great tribulation/punishment, they lost their cultural identities, laws, and commandments of their God. Israel picked up the bad practices and language of the nations where they were scattered.
Ps 84:10. The nation's wicked practices and holidays-(such as Christmas, Thanksgiving, kwanza, etc.) robbed of on people of Israel.

How our God is cleansing Israel his people.

• Ezek 37:1-14, Hos 1:10, Amos 3:1-2. First is the awakening of his people as to who they really are when their punishment draws near to the end. We are not just black, Negro, nigger, African-American, African or any other bywords we have been called in the places where we are scattered among the nations. We are "the sons of the living God". Yes our God is not dead; rather He abandoned us to serve 2000 years punishment for all our errors. Deut 7:6, 14:2. We are the chosen people of our God to serve as his special possession/property.

• Prov 1:23, Ezek 39:29, Ezek 37:5, 9-10, 14, Isa 32:14-15, Rom 8:16. Second, He is pouring out his spirit on his chosen ones as they awaken and accept his reproof/disciplining of them. He then makes His written words known to them, which the nations have not known and have misinterpreted. Israel will then go from being dead and cut off, to be alive because it is the spirit of our God in us that awakens us as a nation/people.

• Dan 12:3-4, John 14:26. Third, with the receiving of the Holy Spirit, the chosen ones with insight will rove about the books-(scriptures) and make true knowledge and understanding of the books abundant to the rest of people. They will bring many to righteousness –doing the right thing as revealed by the spirit through the words of things our God is accomplishing.

• 1Cor15:45-46, John 3:5-8, Mt28:19, Isa 8:16, Joel 2:28, Act 2:17. Fourth, those of Israel who now receive "the spirit of truth of the words/scriptures", who now walk by the spirit's directions of what our God is doing are the disciples and prophets of our God of Israel. They are the born again ones of Israel by the spirit of our God to inherit the kingdom. They will prophesy at the appointed time of what our God is about to do as it the kingdom of heaven draws near to act.

• Deut 28:64, Hos 6:1. Those of Israel who now are born of the spirit and the word of truth will be led by the spirit to separate themselves from the false worships of the gods of the nations. They will return to seeking and worshipping Yahuwah- the God of Israel alone.

Ezek 20:40-44, Deut 30:1-8. These born again people of Israel will be ashamed of our past conducts of leaving our God to go and serve the gods of the nations. Led by the spirit Israel will seek and observe the commandments of our God. However, we will not be perfected while still living in the tent of the wicked until our 2000yrs tribulation ends. Salvation will be granted to the chosen people of God in holy Mount Zion at the end; so we can render sacred service to our God all our life (Lk 169-75).

Rom 8:9-11, 14-17, 29, Isa 54:13. The spirit teaches and helps us to know all the things our God is accomplishing using his son –Yahushua and for him. Through his spirit in us, He will renew our minds as to what He is doing.

Israel is following the path of Yahuwah's judgments

Isa 26:8, 11, Ps 147:19-20. The true people of Israel are following the revealed path of Yahuwah's judgments. These judgments of our God were not revealed to any other nation except Israel.

Isa 26:20. Israel has to follow the path of these judgments until it ends.

What are the paths for His judgments?

Isa 46:8-10. That we may know that He alone is God and there is no one else. His decisions, promises, and councils stand forever and will be carried out.

Gen 15:13-21, Heb 11:6, 9-10. Our God will fulfill his promise to Abraham and his descendant by giving them the Promised Land to inherit forever in their 4th generation in the land.

Hos 5:15. Before Israel will inherit the Promised Land forever, our God will go away and return to his place until Israel bears the punishment for their error.

Hos 6:1-2, 2Pt3:8, Mt 24:21. Israel will be struck/punished for 2days = 2000 years great tribulation.

Hos 3:4-5, Ps 84:10. During the time of this 2000 years final punishment, Israel will dwell for a long time in the tent of wickedness, in the lands/hands of their enemies without a pillar/homeland, a king or prince to gather them together.

Deut 28:64, 68, Lk 21:24. Israel will be scattered among the nations during this judgment time on the nation. Many will be brought again into slavery as done to your forefathers in Egypt. This time by ships as a sign upon your descendants.

Deut 32:35-36. After abandoning, judging and taking vengeance on His people-Israel for 2000yrs. He will save a remnant of them.

Deut 32:37-43, Deut 30:7, Joel 3:2-12. He will then judge the nations for what they did to his people and their land.

Isa 46:13. Our God will grant salvation to the remaining ones of his people in Zion.

Oh, Yahuwah! Our hope is in you.

Isa 26:8, 20, Mt 6:9-10. As we follow the path of your judgments on us, we long for your holy name-Yahuwah to be sanctified, free from all error. The errors are ours and our forefathers to bear the consequences. Please forgive us of our sins against you as we forgive others who sinned against us,

Deliver us from the hands of the wicked. Let your kingdom come at your appointed time and your will be done on earth as in heaven.

Those doing the will of our Father in heaven will enter the kingdom

Why?

Mt 7:21, Mt 25:31-34. "Not everyone saying to me Lord, Lord, will enter into the kingdom of the heavens, but only the one doing the will of my father in heavens will"

Isa 26:8, 20. The will of our God is for all Israel to follow the path of His judgments on us, bear and endure his punishment of us until it ends at the appointed time.

Prov1:23, Heb12:7-11, Lk 15:11-24. His will is that Israel accepts corrections and turn around as the prodigal son did.

John 3:5-8. His will is that Israel will be born again (a new birth) by the spirit before inheriting the kingdom territory forever.

Mt 4:4, Lk 4:4, Jer 31:9, Rom 11:11-12. His will is that all Israel learn from our false steps /mistakes.

Mt 6:33, Lk 12:32. His will is for all Israel to keep seeking first the kingdom and his righteousness...

We must pray according to His revealed Will to be heard at his appointed time.

How?

Isa 26:8. As we –Israel follow the path of your judgments, O Yahuwah, Our hope is in you. We long for your name and your memorial.

Mat6:9. "Your son taught us to pray this way: "' Our Father in the heavens let your name be sanctified, and be free from all error. The blame belongs to us and our forefathers. 10 Please let your Kingdom come. Let your will take place, as in heaven, also on earth.

Isa 46:8-10. We remember this and take courage. We take it to heart, as transgressors. 9 We remember the former things of long ago, that you are God, and there is no other. You are God, and there is no one like you. 10 From the beginning, you foretold the outcome of these events, and from long ago the things that have not yet been done. You said, 'Your decision will stand, and you will do whatever you please.'

Hos 5:15. You said you will go away and return to your place until we bear the consequences of our guilt, and then we will seek your favor. When we are in distress, we will then seek for you."

Hos 3:4-5. You foretold that for a long time your people of Israel will dwell without a king, without a prince, without a sacrifice, without a pillar, and without an ephod and teraphim statues.5 Afterward, the people of Israel will come back and look for Yahuwah their God and for David their king, and they will come trembling to Yahuwah and to his goodness in the final part of the days.

Hos 6:1-2. "We have come looking for you, to return to Yahuwah our God, for you have torn us to pieces, but you will heal us. You struck us, but you will bind our wounds. 2 You promised you will revive us after two days. On the third day, you will restore us and we will live before you.

2Pt3:8. However, we do not let this escape our notice, as your people, that one day with you is as a thousand years and a thousand years elsewhere is as one day.

Ps 84:10. Yes, a day in your courtyards is better than a thousand years anywhere else! We rather choose to stand at the threshold of the house of our God rather than to continue to dwell in the tents of wickedness.

Isa 26:20. However, you have said to us "Go, my people, enter your inner-(prison) rooms And shut your doors behind you. Hide ourselves for a brief moment until your wrath has passed by." You have punished us in your wrath as you desired.

Amos 9:1-10. You have turned your back on us and punished us with great calamities down to this day, month and year of 2019. We have spent nearly 2000yrs years in the tent/land of wickedness, without you and your son our leader ruling over us.

Dan 9:4-5. Now "O Yahuwah the true God, the great and awe-inspiring One, who keeps his covenant and shows loyal love to those who love him and keep his commandments, 5 we have sinned and done wrong and acted wickedly and rebelled; and we have deviated from your commandments and your judgments. 6 We have not listened to your servants the prophets, who spoke in your name to our kings, our princes, our forefathers, and all the people of the land.

Deut 28:64-68. You "Yahuwah have scattered us among all the nations, from the one end of the earth to the other end of the earth, and there we have served gods of wood and of stone, which we and our forefathers have not known. 65 We have no peace among these nations or a place of rest for the sole of our foot. Rather, Yahuwah you have given us there an anxious heart and failing eyes and a feeling of despair. 66 Our lives are in great peril, and we feel dread night and day, and we are uncertain of our survival. 67 In the morning we say, 'If only it were evening!' and in the evening we say, 'If only it is morning!' because of the dread we feel in our hearts and because of what our eyes are seeing. 68 And You Yahuwah have certainly brought us back again into Egypt/slavery by ship, by the way, that you told us, 'We will never see it again,' and in this slavery of 2days = 2000yrs, we have to sell ourselves to our enemies as male and female slaves, but there is no buyer." No one likes us and No one to get us out of it. Rom 9:10. Our eyes became blinded so that we cannot see what has and is happening to us, and we are always made to bend our backs as slaves."

Mt24:21. For nearly 2days/2000yrs we have been in this great tribulation/punishment such as has not occurred since Israel's beginning until now, no, nor will it occur again. 22 The truth is this unless you-our God cut short these days of our punishment, none of us will be saved; but you have said: "on account of your chosen ones those days are cut short" (Deut 32:26-27). For your anger and punishment will not be on us forever.

Heb 12:7. Now oh Yahuwah our God, we need to endure as part of our discipline. You are treating us as sons. For what son is not disciplined by his father? Heb 12:11. True, no discipline seems for the present to be joyous, but it is painful; yet afterward, it yields the peaceable fruit of righteousness to those who have been trained by it.

Dan 9:8-19. "O Yahuwah, to us belong the shame, to our kings, our princes, and our forefathers, because we have sinned against you. 9 To Yahuwah, our God belongs mercy and forgiveness, for we have rebelled against him. 10 We have not obeyed the voice of Yahuwah our God by following his laws that he set before us through his servants the prophets. 11 All Israel has overstepped your Law and turned away by not obeying your voice so that you poured out on us the curse and the sworn oath written about in the Law of Moses the servant of the true God, for we have sinned against Him. 12 He has carried out his words that he spoke against us and against our rulers who ruled over us, by bringing great calamity on us; nothing has ever been done under the whole heavens such as what was done in Jerusalem. 13 Just as it is written in the Law of Moses, this entire calamity has come upon us, yet we have not begged for the favor of Yahuwah our God by turning away from our error and by showing insight into your truth. 14 "So Yahuwah kept watchful and brought calamities on us, for Yahuwah our God is righteous in all the works that he has done; yet we have not obeyed his voice. 15 "Now, O Yahuwah our God, the One who brought your people out of the land of Egypt by a mighty hand and made a name for yourself down to this day, we have sinned and acted wickedly. 16 O Yahuwah, according to all your righteous acts, please, may your anger and wrath turn away from your city Jerusalem, your holy mountain; for because of our sins and the errors of our forefathers, Jerusalem, and your people are an object of reproach to all those around us. 17 And now listen, O our God, to the prayer of your servant and to our entreaties, and cause your face to shine upon your sanctuary that is desolate, for your own sake, O Yahuwah. 18 Incline your ear, O my God, and hear! Do open your eyes and see our desolate condition and the city that has been called by your name; for we are not entreating you because of our righteous acts but because of your great mercy. 19 O Yahuwah, do hear. O Yahuwah, do forgive. O Yahuwah, do pay attention and act! Do not delay, for your own sake, O my God, for your own name has been called upon your city and your scattered people- Israel.

Ezek 37:1-14. Remember O Yahuwah your foretold promise to return in the final days of our tribulation to awaken and restore us from our dead and cut off condition as your people of Israel. Remember your promise to pour out your spirit on all Israel in the last days of our captivity and we will prophesy of your returning to save your inheritance.
Isa 14:1-3, Isa 44:2. Return O Yahuwah to your people. Return to Jeshurun your inheritance. Show us mercy for the sake of your holy name.

Lk 1:69-75. Grant us salvation, and we will serve you and render sacred service to you with the remaining part of our lives.

Isa 46:13. Grant to us the salvation you promised us on your holy Mountain Zion.

Mt 24:29-31. Using Yahushua your son, our Messiah, leader, and king save your scattered people of Israel and rule over us forever (Lk 1:32-33). Amen.

The next ruler ship arrangement for the earth.

Dan 4:17. The declarations of the angels as requested by the holy ones of our God is this: "All people living may know that Yahuwah the God of Israel is ruler in the kingdom of mankind and that He gives the ruling authority to whomever he wants and sets up over it even the lowliest of men"

Dan 4:34. An ancient king of Babylon, Nebuchadnezzar acknowledged the fact that the ruler ship of the Highest God, the one living forever is everlasting and his kingdom is from generation to generation.

Mt 5:45. "Our Father in heaven, the Highest God, makes his sun (favor) shine on both the wicked and the good. He makes it rain on both the righteous and the unrighteous" Yahushua our leader said.

When it comes to the ruling of the earth, the Highest God gives the ruling favors/ privilege to the wicked and also to the righteous. He decides who is giving the ruling authority over the earth and when?

Gen 3:15, John 8:44. The wicked are the human upbringing who choose to side with the devil as ruler and the god they obey. They carry out the will of their father the devil on earth including telling lies to cover their true identity. They even will appear as sheep but they are wolves in sheep clothing.

Rev 12:9, 1John 5:19, Rev 13:9. The devil their father is using the wicked government in his hand to mislead the whole inhabited earth.

Dan 7:25, 2Thess2:3-4, 9-12. The wicked, man of lawlessness, will stand in opposition and exalt himself/his kind of ruler ship above everything called god or object of worship. Yes, the wicked governments in the hands of the devil will oppose /challenge every rulings and decision of the true God.

Dan 2:37-43, Rev 13:4, Job 9:24, Ps 71:4, Jer 15:21, Ezek 7:21, Lk 21:24. God allowed for four wild beasts with the authority of the devil to rise up on the earth and rule it. The devil gave its authority to the wicked – (his loyal wife-like human offspring) the favor to rise and rule, and trample the earth for an appointed time. This fulfills the things God foretold from the beginning at Gen 3:15, Isa 46:10.

Ps 97:10, Ps 82:4, 1Pt 1:2-5. However, God will at the end rescue His loyal wife-like human off springs after her been bruised by the devil's off springs.

Act 2:23-24, Acts 3:15, Lk 1:32-33. After being bruised by the wicked, God rescued Yahushua-the one He chose to rule as king over His loyal wife-like offspring-Israel. He will also rescue His loyal wife-like offspring from the hand of the wicked after she has being humiliated and bruised for an appointed time Ezek 39:21-29.

The ruling government in the hands of the righteous.

Gen 3:15. God will restore his loyal human off springs, who will chose him and obey him as their God and obey his ruling over them.

Gen 15:13-21. He Chose Abraham and his chosen offspring –Israel to be the source of establishing the ruler ship over the earth by the righteous at the appointed time.

Dan 2:44, Dan 7:12. In the final days/ time given as a favor to the wicked to rule the earth, Yahuwah will set up a kingdom government over the earth. This righteous government will put to an end every other ruling government on earth.

Dan 7: 13-14, 22, 27, Mt 19:28, Rev 20:4, Rev 5:10. The righteous ruler ship over the earth will be in the hand of Yahushua-the son of God and his chosen ones (the holy ones of Israel).

Isa 9:6-7, Lk 1:32-33, Dan 9:26. The king and leader for a righteous ruler ship over the earth will be cut off-bruised for a while by the human off springs of the devil- wicked governments ruling the earth. (Ps 2:1-3).

2Thess 1:6-10, Acts 3:21. However, He will return with his powerful angels at the appointed time by God to crush all other ruling government on earth and then establish his righteous government on the earth.

Zech 8:1-8, Isa 46:13, Rev 21:1-6. The headquarters for God's righteous government over the earth will be in Zion, Jerusalem. Not in London, New York, Washington DC, Moscow or Shanghai. Every other government/kingdom will submit to our God – Yahuwah and the king Yahushua in Zion (Zech 14:16, Rev 21:24-26, Ps 2:10-12)

Zech 14:3-17, Joel 3:2-6, 9-21. The Kings, the governments, and the armies of the wild beasts were all given advanced notice by the true God to be ready for war over Zion in the valley of Jehoshaphat.

Do not take on the mark of the wild beast.

Dan2:37-43, Rev 13:16-18. These wild beasts were permitted by God to rise successively and rule the earth for an appointed time. For example, the last two wild beasts was allowed to rule and trample the holy place and its people for a period of 2300 days and nights (Dan 8:13-14).

What is a mark?

Ezek 9:4, Rev 13:17, 2Thess 3:14. A mark can be an identification sign, symbol, Ideology, or characteristic used to identify an object as a part of a collective group. Many try to focus on a numerical symbol (666) to identify the mark of the beast the chosen people are asked not to take on or be part of. Thus they neglect the characteristic mark of the beast.

What is the characteristic mark of the wild beast government?

• Ps 2:1-3. They are antichrist/ Yahushua. In opposition to him ruling the earth.

• Deut 32:7-9, Deut 7:6, 14:2, Rev 13:6-8, Dan 7:25, 2Thess 2:3-4. They are anti-god. In opposition to the rulings and decisions of the true God.

• Rev 13:4-5, 11-18. They are of the wicked the devil. Their goal is to unite and rule all peoples as one humanity under the dragon- devil's authority. Anyone not accepting their goal/mark is to be killed and will not do business with the wild beast economics system.

• Rev 13:8. Cause all people to worship and serve the wild beast and receive its mark as being part of the beast. E.g. 501c mark exempts a group from paying taxes to the beast but the group still has the mark of the beast by promoting the agenda/plans of the beast. W2 mark shows a person is in compliance with the wild beast but that does not mean worshiping and serving the wild beast (Mt 17:24-27). Your voter registration card shows your support and participation in the wild beast system, even worshiping and praising it as the best there is (Rev 13:4, 8). All other people on earth will worship and serve the wild beast except the chosen Israelites whose names are in the lamb's book of life. They know that taking the mark of the beast/being part of the beast is against the plans and decisions of the true God (Ps 2:1-12).

Why reject the mark of the wild beast?

Jam 4:4. Friendship with the world (of the wild beast) is enmity with the true God. Whosoever wants to go along with the world is making himself an enemy of God. Therefore, by accepting the mark of the wild beast, it marks one as rejecting the true God and his son from ruling over them.

John 17:14-19, John 15:19, John 18:36. The chosen ones of Israel are to be no part of this world/beast system. Just as our God and King is no part of this wild beast system. Yes, the chosen ones are in the world but they are to be set apart/ sanctified until the wild beast appointed times ends. The righteous government of our God is no part of this present wild beast system (Dan 2:44).

Rev 13:12-14. It is important that you identify the characteristic marks of the beast in order not to go along worshiping and associating with the economical, religious and political mark of the wild beast system.

Rev 13:18. The total system of the wild beast (its political, religious and economical, etc.) is not perfect because it is of a man's number (666). The chosen ones of Israel are to keep seeking first the kingdom of God that will usher in a perfect righteous ruling of the earth at God's appointed time.

What will happen to those who accepted the mark and worshiped/served the beast?

Mt 24:4-5, 24, Rev 12:9, Rev13:4-8, 12-14, Rev 21:27. The devil will use the wild beast to deceive all who dwell on the earth to worship him as god. Except those whose names are written in the lamb's book of life. That is the chosen ones of Israel to receive the kingdom of God.

Rev 14:9-12, Ps 75:8, Rev 21:8. The cowards and those without faith who went along with worshiping and serving the wild beast instead of seeking the kingdom of God; their portion will be in the lake of fire of destruction.

Are you a lawless worker or a lawful worker in the vineyard?

Mt 21:28-32. A father-(God) has two sons- (Israel and Judah). Israel said no to doing the father's will, Judah said he will do the father's will but did not do it. The lesson is that the father is looking for his sons to make his heart rejoice by doing as He asked Mt4:4.

Mt 21:33-41. A lawful worker will cultivate the master's vineyard at appointed times and return the yield to the master. However, an evil slave/lawless worker will be seeking his own interest ignoring any instructions/directions from the master.
Mt13:24-30. A man-(God) sends his two sons to sow fine seed in his field/vineyard. While men were sleeping his enemy came and over sowed it with weeds-(lawless workers) who planted fake seeds in the field.

Who is the worker of lawlessness?

Mt7:21-22. A worker or servant who does not know the goal, plan, and directions of the master to accomplish his work. This person is just working to satisfy his ego, interest, and satisfaction at the end. This is a person working in a field/vineyard that does not belong to him.

Jn 10:1, 10. The lawless one enters the sheepfold/vineyard through a back door. Like a thief, he sneaks in at night when men are sleeping or inattentive. In the morning he makes himself as one of the workers (sons)
The lawless worker is gathering sheep to follow after himself.

Mt13:39. The enemy who planted the weeds-lawless workers in the vineyard is the devil.

The master's reply/reward at the end for the lawless workers.

Mt 7:23. "I never knew you, or I did not send you, depart from me you workers of lawlessness!"
Mt 13:39-42. He will send His angels at the conclusion of this system and they will collect out from his kingdom/vineyard all things causing stumbling and people who practice lawlessness (lawless workers).

Who is a lawful worker?

John 5:17. A worker or servant that knows the goal, plan, and directions given by the master to accomplish his work. The lawful workers sent into the field are from Judah and Israel not from other nations. Any other workers are drawing sheep of Israel after themselves.

John 10:11-18. Yahushua is the fine shepherd/lawful worker with the goal, plan, and directions from the father regarding his vineyard/kingdom.

John 6:44, John 15:16, Mt 20:1-16. Yahushua and his father also hire/chooses other lawful workers to send to work in the field. The lawful workers are hired at different hours to fit into the master's plan, goal, and directions.

Ezek 36:5-16, Ezek 37:1-14, Hos 6:1-2, Mt 10:1-42 . The lawful workers have the master's goal, plan and appointed times and directions to follow until the work is completed.

The master's reply/reward at the end to the lawful workers.

Mt 20:8-9, Mt 25:19-23, Mt 24:45-47. The faithful lawful workers will be rewarded and appointed over the master's belonging-vineyard/kingdom at the master's return.

Why do we need to know the goal, plan, and direction of the master?

• To ensure we are following his directions to achieve his goal.
• To use his appointed times to pace ourselves to complete the work.

• To ensure we are working according to his plan to earn his satisfaction at the end.
Mt 20:1-4, Mt 25:14-15, Lk 21:20-22. The master never sends out his lawful workers into the field without giving them the goal, plan, and directions to get the work done.

What is His name?

Exod 3:6-13. Moses wants to know the name of the true God of Abraham to declare to Abraham's descendants that are in slavery in Egypt to call on for their salvation and deliverance.

Exo 12:40-41, Gal 3:17, Gen 15:13, Jer 25:14. For more than 200 years of 430 years of Abraham's descendants so journeying in the land of Canaan and Egypt, they were subjected to slavery position with hard labor in the land of Egypt.

Deut 32:7, Gen 15:13-21. Their ancestors must have told them of their history, how the true God appeared to their ancestor Abraham and the promise he received from God. They must have told them how the true God protected Abraham and provided deliverance for him and how He led them to sojourn into Egypt. They must have told them how the true God has protected and provided for them all of these times.

However, this generation that is now in bondage in Egypt must be wondering and asking, where is the God of their forefather Abraham? Why is it that He has not appeared to deliver them as He promised to Abraham? Moreover, oppression must have caused many to forget the name and the God of their ancestors and take to seeking the gods of their oppressing nation since they are in power over them.

Therefore, when Moses asked the true God what he is to say to the suffering Abraham's descendants in Egypt, he was asking a reasonable question that will help them to separate from seeking the false gods of Egypt and help them to know the name of the true God that the people need to call on for their deliverance and salvation from the hand of the Egyptians.

The true God revealed his name and the power behind that name to Moses to give to the descendants of Abraham to call on (pray to). Moses is to tell them what the true God is about to do on their behalf; that is to deliver them from the hands of the Egyptians.

Before Israel's final destruction in A.D.70.

John 17:6, 26, Mt6:9. Isa 26:8. Act 2:21. Yahushua, the greater than Moses, made the name of God of Israel, the only true God known to the chosen ones of Israel to call on for their salvation from the destruction coming upon the nation.

Acts 2:38, 5:28, Lk 1:32-33, 69-75. The disciples also declared that there is no salvation and forgiveness of sins for Israelites from the judgment/vengeance of

God upon them except in the name of Yahushua who came from the father. Until today, Israel is yet to be granted salvation and forgiveness from our sins (Mt 23:39. Isa 46:13, Isa 14:1-3).

Hos 3:4-5, Hos 5:15, Hos 6:1-2, 2Pt 3:8. The judgment/punishment upon Israel will last for 2000 years after which Israel's salvation will be granted in Zion.

Fast forward to present day 2019.

The chosen descendants of Abraham-Israel have been in nearly 2000yrs tribulation/punishment scattered among the nations of the earth. Many are wondering, why are there so many afflictions on them? What have they done to deserve such? Where is the God of their ancestors, does He not see what is been done to them and how pitiful their condition is? Does He not see the wickedness of the people He has put over them?

Exo 28:64. Many have forgotten who the God of their ancestors is. Many are deceived into calling on and serving the gods of other nations. Others have forgotten their true ancestral origin -Israel and have taken the identity of the nations or countries where they were scattered or now reside. They call on the gods of other peoples thinking that they can get relief from the judgment of the true God on them.

Ezek 37:1-14, Gen 15:16, Joel 3:6-21. The God of Abraham promised to awaken his chosen people of Israel in the final part of their days of punishment among the nations. He will bring them home, back to their promised land.

Hos 6:1-2, Prov1:23, Ezek 39:29. He will pour out his holy spirit on those of Israel ancestry who accepted his 2days reproof /discipline of them and turned around. He will make his words known to such ones. Isa 43:1-8, Ezek 39:7. God of Abraham will make his name known again to his chosen ones. So that the chosen ones will call on his name for their salvation and deliverance from among the oppressing nations.

Ezek 20:36-39, Isa 10:20-23, Amos 9:10-12. However, not all with Israel ancestry will make it back to the promised land-(the kingdom). Those who chose to keep serving and call on the gods of the nations will not.

Gen 15:16 Act 2:21, Lk 1:32-33, 69-75, Mt 24:29-31. God of Abraham will send the messiah and deliverer-Yahushua at the appointed time to lead his chosen ones out from among the nations back to the Promised Land to inherit it forever. Those calling on (praying to) and trusting in His name for their foretold salvation.

Deut 32:36-43, Isa 8:7-11.Ezek 39:21-29, Ezek 38:16, Mal 1:11. God of Abraham will once again display his power and execute judgment; this time among the nations where His chosen ones are scattered. He will act to deliver them out and prove Himself as their God and savior. Gog- the leader of the nations and Magog- the nations that came against Israel will all receive their judgment of destruction when our God rises to execute judgment on behalf of his chosen people.

Why does the wicked one keep stealing?

Mt 13:18-19, John 10:10, 1Pt 5:8. The thief will come to steal, kill and destroy the property inheritance of Abraham's offspring with the promise.

Who is the wicked one?

Mt 13:25, 28, 39. The enemy, the wicked one, and the devil is a man. He is the one called the devil who planted his seed or off springs to lay claim of the inheritance of God's loyal wife-like offspring- Israel.

How can we identify this man?

Mt 7:20. By their fruits, you will identify these men. By the things they have done or their works, you will know which people fit the tree/man or character called the devil.

The kingdom territory is promised to Abraham and his off spring-Israel.

Gen 15:13-21, Mt 13:24-28. The Promised Land is for Abraham and his descendant to inherit it in their 4th generation in the land. Then they will possess it forever.

1John 5:19. However, the wicked one came, stole and took over the Promised Land. The wicked one persecuted the true sons of the kingdom, scattering them far away from the land territory. The wicked one planted his seed in the kingdom territory and completely took over the land.

Mt 13:19, Mt 6:33. When a true Hebrew Israelite hears the word of the kingdom and does not get the meaning of it; the wicked one comes and snatches it away so that they do not inquire anymore of it or seek to return back to it. That way the kingdom territory that was stolen by the wicked still stays in the possession of the sons of the wicked one. The wicked one comes and steals, changes the true meaning/sense of the word so that the true sons of the kingdom continue in lack of knowledge and therefore perish for lack of knowledge. Even during the messiah's time on earth, the wicked one has already planted his seed persecuting the true sons to inherit the kingdom territory.

The decision of our God still stands.

Gen 15:16-21, Isa 46:10, Ps 33:10-12. Our God will give the kingdom territory to Abraham's descendant-Israel to possess forever in their 4th generation in the land.

Mt 13:30, Amos 9:11-13. Until the harvest time in the conclusion of the system.

Isa 65:8-10. The kingdom territory will be given to Israelites who hear the word of the kingdom, search and seek to return to it. The sons of the wicked one will be uprooted and destroyed away from the land.

Mt 25:34. The chosen Israelites, blessed by the father will inherit the kingdom territory prepared for them from the founding of the world.

Mic 5:8. Until then the chosen ones of Israel to inherit the kingdom will be as the lion in the midst of the beasts of the forest. Wait patiently until it is the father's appointed time to give them the kingdom.

Dan 7:23-27, Dan 8:25, 2Thess 1:6-10. The destroying and removing of the wicked one from the kingdom territory will be accomplished not with a human hand. Yahushua and his angels will do that at his return.

What will happen to those whose knowledge or word of the kingdom was stolen by the devil?

Hos 4:6. They will perish for lack of knowledge.

Act1:7, Isa 10:21-23, Amos 9:10-12, Ezek 20:36-38. These will be exterminated in the final judgment by our God before the restoration and recreation of the kingdom.

In the time for the resurrection of the dead.

Ezek 37:1-14, John 5:25-29. Yahuwah the God of Israel foretold that He will resurrect the whole house of Israel after He abandons them for a long time. Yahushua stated, "The hour is coming and it is now. The dead will hear his voice and come back to life."

Who are the dead?

Deut 32:35-36. It was foretold that God will judge his people of Israel. During the time of their judgment and punishment, the nation Israel will become a dead nation, put out of existence.

Hos 3:4-5. For a long time (2000yrs), Israel will cease to exist (put to death) as a nation following their messiah and leader that was cut off/put to death. Israel will have no king, no prince, no pillar-(homeland), no ephod and no teraphim statue (God to defend them)

Rev 11:18. The nations became wrathful and they put Israel to death. Then came the wrath of God of Israel, and time for the dead-(Israel) to be raised up /resurrected first, and time for their reward and judgment of those ruining the earth. The sequence of these God scheduled events shows that the resurrecting of the nation Israel will take place first before the complete destruction of those ruining the earth.

Why did God put Israel to death?

Hos 5:15, Hos 6:1-2, 2Pt 3:8. God will return to his place in heaven until the people of Israel bear the punishment for all their errors. Israel's punishment will be for 2days = 2000 years among the nations.

Will it be a resurrection to inherit life or resurrection of final judgment /second death?

Hos 1:10. In many lands where people of Israel were scattered they were told that they are nobody, gentiles, etc., However, in the final part of their exile for punishment, during the awakening or resurrection time, they will be told that they are the sons of the living God of Israel.

Ezek 20:36-38, Isa 10:21-23, Amos 9:10-12. Some will be awakened/resurrected and judged as not fit to return back to the kingdom territory of God. This is because of their works of conduct.
• Denying what their true identity is.
• Refusing to seek first the kingdom but kept seeking vain things.

- Isa 8:18-19. Refusing to leave the worshipping of false gods of the nations and seek and return to their God.
- Rejecting discipline by refusing to go in by the narrow gate leading to life.
- Lack of faith in the kingdom restoration message. Rev 21:8. For all the above conducts, many Israelites will be judged unfit to return back to the kingdom in the time of resurrection. Those considered unfit will be condemned to a second death (Isa 10:21-23). Few awakened Israelites will be judged as fit for life in the kingdom because of their conduct after they were awakened/resurrected.
- Prov 1:23, Heb12:6-11, Mt 4:17. They accepted reproof of their God and repented of their error.
- Exo 28:64, Ezek 20:32, 39, Isa 8:13. They stopped seeking and serving gods of other nations.
- Hos 6:1, Deut 30:1-8. They searched and returned to calling on the name of Yahuwah their God.
- Mt 6:33. They kept seeking first the kingdom and his righteousness.
- They exercised faith in the things written.
- Rev 2:11, Mt 7:13-14. They endured in the narrow road that leads to life in the kingdom. Ezek 20:37, Rev 20:6. These are judged by their conduct after their resurrection as fit for life in the kingdom of God. These will not experience the second death (Isa 10:21-23) on all Israel but will serve as priests of God and Yahushua, and will rule with him for the 1000 years.

Have faith in the faithful God!

Mt 4:4, 10, 1Pt 1:16. Rom 3:4, Mt 26:31. If Yahushua is present today, He will be pointing out scriptures to encourage us by saying it is written. All things recorded in the scriptures must be fulfilled. This is because His father, our God will carry out whatever decisions He has made, even his counsels of long ago (Isa 46:8-10).

The God that is faithful.

Gen 15:13-21, Isa 45:21, Ps 33:11. Yahuwah is the God who is faithful to all His promises. All the things that He foretold that would befall the descendants of Abraham his friend will be carried out faithfully. This is so that we may know that He alone is God and there is no one else.

Isa 46:8-10, Isa 42:9. He foretold from long ago the things that have occurred, is occurring at present and things that will be carried out soon regarding Abraham's descendant-Israel.

The Records of his faithfulness.

• Gen 15:13, Jer 25:14. He foretold that many nations will enslave the offspring of Abraham. However, after He will deliver them and prove Himself their God.

He did deliver Israel from Egypt, Babylon, med Persia, and Greece.

• Deut 28:64. He foretold He will scatter Israel among the nations and there they will serve false God of the nations.

Lk 21:24. Since AD 70, the people of Israel have been in exile, scattered among the nations; even till today, they are among the nations serving false gods of other nations.

• Hos 5:15, 6:1-2, 2Pt 3:8. He foretold He will go away and Israel will bear the punishment for 2days = 2000 years.

Mt 23:37-39. Since AD 33, the nation of Israel became abandoned by their God and removed from the Promised Land. Israel is bearing punishment among the nations until it ends.

• Exod 28:68. He foretold that He would bring the descendants of Israel again into Egypt (slavery) with ships because of their breaking away from the covenant.

The trans-Atlantic slave trade of Israel offspring that fled into Africa proves that He did carry out whatever He said He will do.

• 2Chron 36:20-21. He foretold that He would bring Israel into Babylon bondage and will bring them out after 70 years of their captivity in Babylon.

Ezra 1:1-2. After serving 70 years, our God did free his people and faithfully brought Israel out of Babylon.

The records of our God faithfully carrying out all his decisions and things He foretold are so many to recount them all.

His future promises.

Hos 6:1-2. 2Pt 3:8, Mt 24:29-31. After 2days =2000 years of tribulation/punishment, our God foretold that He will return to gather Israel back and raise them up on the third day.

Isa 26:20. He foretold that Israel would enter their inner rooms (prison cells) and serve their punishment until his anger ends.

Isa 14:3. He foretold that He would show mercy to Jacob would once again choose Israel and restore them in their land.

Rev20:6, Ps 45:16. He foretold that chosen sons of Israel would receive authority to rule with their messiah and leader for 1000yrs over the earth.

Prov 3:5. Trust in Yahuwah with all your heart, have faith in him to fulfill all his promises. He will do what He said He would do.

Awakened /resurrected ones of Israel have to endure until the appointed time for restoring the kingdom.

Ezek 37:1-14. Our God foretold that He will resurrect the whole house of Israel in the final part of their being dead and cut off due to the tribulations/punishment on them.

Hos 5:15, Hos 6:1-2, 2Pt 3:8. The punishment on Israel will last for 2days =2000 years.
Mt 23:37-39, Mt 27:46. Yahuwah began the abandoning of Israel and went away in the year AD 33.

When is the appointed time of the end of the punishment on Israel?

AD 33 +2000 years = year AD 2033.
Mt 24:32:35, Lk 21:29-33, Mt 24:13. Therefore, awakened/resurrected ones of Israel have to endure until the year 2033 for their salvation and deliverance.

Mt 10:22, Deut 32:36-43, Ezek 3. The chosen ones of Israel will be hated by all people on account of their

God's name (God of vengeance) however they have to endure until the end to be saved.

Joel 2:28-29, Mt 10:5-42. The chosen ones will be hated by all peoples on account of their prophesying about the end of all things, about the kingdom of heaven drawing near to execute the next scheduled event regarding the kingdom territory of God.

The final day or the final hour?

Act 1:6-7. The first-century disciples of our God were not given the privilege of understanding the full times and seasons that the father has scheduled within Him. However, they were given knowledge of the next event to come by the messiah, our leader.

Mt 24:36-42. Concerning the exact day and final hour countdown of the end of the punishment on Israel and the beginning of their deliverance and restoration, nobody knows except our God alone.

The road marker or signpost.

Jer 31:21. Our God asked his chosen ones (the 5 wise virgins/bride maids) to setup road markers or signposts to know when and how close the return to their kingdom cities are.

Mt 24:29-31. Our Messiah gave us a road marker; He assured us that "Immediately the tribulation/punishment of those days on Israel ends, the sign of the son of man will be seen in the heaven, signaling his return to gather back his chosen ones. The chosen ones of Israel will be gathered from the four corners of the earth by the angels of our God.

Isa 8:17, Mt 24:32-42. We must keep in expectation of our God to return and carry out his words, things He foretold from long ago (Gen 15:13-21). That is to give to Abraham's Descendants-Israel the kingdom territory to possess forever in their 4th generation. Not one of his words will pass away or be thrown away without fulfilling it.

Dan 7:13-14, 27, Mt 28:18, 1Cor 15:24-28. Yahushua the son of God, our leader and king has been given all authority in heaven and earth to execute and fulfill all of God's decisions and His will of long ago. These decisions he will carry out at our God's appointed times for them to be fulfilled starting with the awakening and resurrecting of those who belong to him (chosen ones of Israel) Lk1:32-33, 69-75.

The will of the living God.

Mt 6:9-10, Isa 46:8-10

What is a will?

A will is a written legal document or spoken word stating the desired decisions and actions to be executed on behalf of an entity or a person.
Example. A parent may have a living that will be executed if they are not able to do so. The will may contain parent's decision on which children are to inherit what property.

What is in God's written will?

Gen 15:13-21. The descendant of Abraham-Israel will inherit the promised kingdom territory forever in their 4th generation in the land.

Dan 2:44, Dan7:13-14. The chosen ones of Israel (holy ones) will receive a kingdom that will never be destroyed or passed on to any other people...

Ps 2:6-10, Lk 1:32-33. God's son Yahushua will rule as king over them forever in the kingdom of their God and father. The nations and peoples of the earth will be subjected to Him and his government established in Zion, Jerusalem.

Lk 1:69-75, Ps45:16, Rom 9:4 Rev 20:6, 1Pt 2:9. The remaining chosen survivals of Israel will render sacred service to our God in his kingdom and serve as priests and kings in all the earth.

Gen 3:15. God's loyal wife-like government in the hands of his son will crush and put to an end the devil's established government on earth.

The blessings of the kingdom of our God.

Rev 22:1-2, Ezek 47:12, Rev 22:14. The river of life with the water of life and trees for the healing of the nations will be in the city of the restored kingdom of our God.

Rev 22:3-4. No longer will there be any curse on the people of Israel. The chosen ones, slaves of our God will render to him sacred service and behold his face. This is because the anger of God on his people will have ended.

Deut 7:6, Deut 14:2, Rom 9:4, Rev 20:6, Lk 1:69-75. The privilege of rendering sacred service to the true God belongs to the People of Israel alone; they are Yahuwah's chosen ones to serve Him. It does not belong to any other people since the decision of God still stands.

Rev 22:5, John 10:10. No more will there be the night for the nation of Israel. That is no more will Israel be removed from their land, put out of existence by the thief that came at night to steal God's sheep, treasures and inheritance, kill and destroy the Nation-Israel.

Amos 9:15, Jer 31:40, Gen 15:13-21. Our God will plant Israel on their land and we will never again be uprooted from the land that Yahuwah has given to us.

Prov 12:3, Isa 60:21, Ezek34:27-28, Ezek 37:23-25. Israel will be a righteous sprout planted by Yahuwah our God. We will possess the land forever as He promised to Abraham.

Isa 8:10, Ps 46:5-11, Rev 21:3-4, Mt1:21-23. Another blessing the kingdom will bring is that God, our God will dwell with his people Israel. Despite the plans of the nations, God will save his people from their sins, cleanse them and establish his kingdom with them and dwell with them.

Exod 20:6, Mt 4:4. The blessings of the kingdom will last for up to 1000 generations (forever) if we love our God and keep his commandment.
Isa 49:20, John 14:18. Israel will not be left bereaved forever but will be comforted by our God with many sons to expand the kingdom territory.

We are in the world but not really part of this world.

John 17:16. "They are no part of the world, just as I am no part of the world."

What is this world?

1John 5:19. We originated with God. Yahuwah our God is the one that created Israel to produce a righteous kingdom of kings and priests to rule the earth. However, this present world system of Esau, Romans, Caucasian ruler ship is in the hand of the wicked.

Mt 5:45, Job 9:24. Our God is giving favor to both the wicked and the righteous to take turns to rule the earth.

John 18:36. Therefore, since we- Israel and our king is no part of this world under Satan- the devil ruler ship, "we are no part of this world". The devil and his chosen people will continue to rule this wicked system until the appointed time granted to them by our God.

Dan 2:44, Dan 7:13-14, 28, 2Thess 1:6-10. However, our world will begin after the world in the hands of the wicked one ends.

The world that the holy ones are waiting for.

Heb 11:10. A world /kingdom having real foundations, whose designer and builder is God.
Heb12:7-10, 1Pt1:15-16. Holy ones are in training, receiving discipline that we may partake of his holiness and righteousness in His kingdom/world to come.

2Pt 3:13, Mt 6:33. Holy ones are seeking and looking forward to a new world of a new heaven and earth wherein righteousness dwells.
Isa 9:7. A world established with justice and righteousness.

Isa 32:1, Rev 19:11. A world in which a king will rule for righteousness and carry on a war in righteousness.

Requirements for surviving and entering into the new world.

Zeph 2:3. Observe our God's righteous decrees, seek righteousness, and seek meekness.

Prov 1:23, Heb12:11, Hos 6:1-2. Accept the discipline meant for the holy ones. Holy ones of Israel are in a 2days =2000yrs discipline in order to produce fruits of righteousness fit for the new world.

Isa 48:18. By paying attention to the commandments and instructions of our God, the righteousness of the holy ones will flow like the wave of the sea.

Mt 4:4, Ezek 18:20. Holy ones will live by observing every utterance from the mouth of our God. The soul that sins will die, that is righteousness.

Mt 5:6, 1Tim 6:11. Those hungering and thirsting for righteousness will be satisfied in the new world to come.

The rewards of seeking and pursuing righteousness.

Heb 11:33. Through faith in our God's promises, those pursuing righteousness have defeated/overcame kingdoms, brought about righteousness, and obtained promises.

For example: In the 1st century, those seeking and pursuing righteousness through faith in our God's promises overcame the death of the nation of Israel, obtained the promise to rule as kings in the righteous kingdom of Yahushua to come (Lk 22:28-30, Jam 1:18, Rom 8:23).

Ezek 37:1-14, Act 15:14-18. Through faith in our God's promises, we the chosen ones in the final days of Israel's punishment, who are seeking the righteousness of the promised kingdom, can obtain the promises as final fruits harvested from among the nations for the righteous kingdom of our God.

Our God will do the things He promised at His scheduled appointed times.

Why?

Num 23:19. God is not a man who tells lies, nor the son of a man who changes his decisions.

Ps 89:35. He has sworn in his holiness for the last time. He said He will not tell lies to David.
Tit 1:2. ".. Based on a hope of the everlasting life that God, who cannot lie, promised long ago.

1Sam 15:29. "Moreover, the Excellency of Israel will not prove false or change his mind, for He is not a mere man that he should change his mind." Yes, He will not change his mind in the things He has revealed He will do regarding his chosen sons of Israel (Isa 43: 1-8, Isa 45:11).

Isa 14:24. Yahuwah of armies has sworn; "just as I have intended, so it will occur. And just as I have decided, that is what will come true."

Isa 46:10. "From the beginning, I foretell the outcome, and from long ago the things that have not yet been done. I say my decision will stand, and I will do whatever I please."

Mic 7:20. "Yahuwah will show faithfulness to Jacob, loyal love to Abraham, As He swore to our forefathers from the days of old.

Things our God will soon carry out at his appointed times.

Gen 15:13-21. He promised to give the territory He swore to Abraham and his descendant to inherit forever in their 4th generation in the land.

Isa 14:3. He will show mercy to Jacob and will again choose Israel. He will restore them to their land after their punishment time of hard slavery among the nations ends.

Hos 6:1-2, 2Pt 3:8. The punishment /tribulation on Israel will last for 2days = 2000 years.

Isa 65:6-7. Israel will receive her punishment/ tribulation in the full measure before our God will let his people who have not searched for him to find him and receive his mercy and salvation.

Full measure = until completion of punishment time or sentence.

Isa 26:8, 20. Israel will follow the path of His judgments and enter into their inner/prison rooms until his anger has ended. Israel will be hidden, cutoff during this appointed time of their punishment.

Ezek 37:1-14. At the appointed time in the final part of the days, our God will pour out his holy spirit and awaken his people of Israel. He will get the chosen ones ready for gathering back to the Promised Land. Isa 46:13, Lk 1:69-75. Our God will grant salvation to Israel in Zion at the end of our punishment.

Isa 10:21-23, Amos 9:10-12. Though the number of the people of Israel multiple as the sand of the sea, only a few remnants will return to the mighty God. Extermination has been decided on for the rest in the day for our God to raise up the booth of David that is fallen...

Zech 8:1-8, Rev 21:3-4. Our God will return to Zion and will restore it as in the days of long ago. He will restore the place of his footstool and dwell with his people –Israel.

Will you search for the instructions and directions of our God? Will you keep in expectation of Him?

Ps 32:8, Isa 8:17. Our God promised to give to his chosen ones insight and instruct them in the way they should go. He will give advice with his eye upon them. His eye will be on us to see if we are obediently following his directions and instructions.

If we are obedient and attentive.

Ps 119:105. His word will be a lamp to our feet and a light to our roadway/path. It will keep shinning to show us where we are standing in the stream of time and how far more to go to get to our destination – Zion.

Isa 26:8. His words will reveal to us the path of his judgments we are to follow until the end.
Mt 6:9-10. If we are seeking for the sanctification of his holy name, He will show mercy to us at the end of our 2000years punishment/tribulation.

Ezek 37:1-14. He will awaken the whole house of Israel in the final part of the days of our punishment/tribulation.

Joel 2:28-29, Prov 1:23, Ezek 39:29. He will pour out his spirit on us and make his words- (what is written) known to us. He will give us an understanding of his activities of long ago and that which is to come.

Isa 32:14-15, Acts 2:16-20, 38-39. We will then prophesy at the appointed time given of our God drawing near to execute the next foretold and scheduled event concerning Abraham's chosen offspring –Israel.

The wilderness/desolated land and people of Israel will become an orchard again; the orchard will become a beautiful forest full of trees of righteousness again.

Isa 44:3-5, John 14:16-18, 1Cor 2:12. The Holy Spirit is a promise only to the descendant of Jacob/Israel. It is not for any other people.

Mt 4:1. Yahushua was full of and led by the Holy Spirit of God. He was taught by the father and then was tested.

Amos 9:1-4, Dan 9:26, Isa 53:1-8. At the appointed time of 3.5 years prior to the next event; Time for the Messiah, the chief cornerstone of Israel to be cut off. Yahushua started ministering and saying "Repent for the kingdom of heavens has drawn near" for the execution of the next scheduled event concerning his chosen people of Israel.

Acts 1:7-8. Yahushua stated that the chosen ones for his kingdom would receive power when the holy spirit of God is poured out for us and we are to be witnesses of him in Jerusalem, in all Judea, Samaria and most distant part of the earth.

Amos 9:10-12, Lk 1:32-33, Mt 1:21. We are to bear witness of him as the chosen one to save and restore the booth of David that has fallen. Just as a generation of Israel witnessed the acts of our God as he delivered Israel out of Egypt with a mighty hand. The first-century disciples received the gift of the spirit and did bear witness of his death and all the things the messiah taught them will come upon the nation- Israel after his death (Amos 9:1-4, John 8:28, Mt 23:37-39, Mt 24:2, Lk 21:24, Lk 23:28).

All did take place to fulfill Yahushua's foretold word at Mt 24:35 "heavens and earth will pass away, but my words will by no means pass away or be discarded and go unfulfilled.

Hos 6:2, Mt 24:21 Jam 1:27, Mt 24:9, Rom12:12, 2Thess 1:6-10. They are witnesses of Israel's destruction and the tribulation that will follow the people of Israel until the end of their 2days =2000 years punishment.

Ezek 37:1-14, Hos 6:1-3, Deut 32:36, Ezek 39:21-29. However, our God foretold that in the final part of the days of Israel's punishment and tribulation judgment, He will again pour out his gift of Holy Spirit on the descendants of Jacob. They will be witnesses of our God and messiah-Yahushua as they carry out the foretold actions to awaken Israel from the dead and cutoff condition to their restoration back to their promised homeland.

Amos 3:7, Hab 2:3, Isa 46:11. The chosen ones in the final part of the days will prophesy 3.5 years prior to the appointed time of the end of punishment and the beginning of a new event as revealed/foretold by our God.

Who are the witnesses of Yahuwah the God of Israel?

Isa 43:1, 10. 1 "Now this is what Yahuwah says, Your Creator, O Jacob, the One who formed you, O Israel: "Do not be afraid, for I have repurchased you. I have called you by your name. You belong to me.""

10 "You are my witnesses," declares Yahuwah, "Yes, my servant whom I have chosen, So that you may know and have faith in me, and understand that I am the same One. Before me, no God was formed, and after me, there has been none".

Therefore, generations of the offspring of Jacob/Israel are the witnesses to the activities of Yahuwah the God of Abraham. Witnesses to the things He is doing to faithfully carry out the promise He made to Abraham his friend at Gen 15:13-21.

How?

Gen15:13-21, Isa 45:21, Amos 9:11-12, Acts 15:15-18, Baruch2:30-35. Yahuwah made a promise to Abraham, that He will give the lands mentioned in Gen 15:13-21 to the descendants of Abraham to inherit forever in their 4th generation in the land. Since then, Yahuwah God has been working to carry out things towards fulfilling that promise.

Exod12:28-33. Israel witnessed the mighty hands of Yahuwah as he delivered our ancestors from bondage to the Egyptians. They witnessed the destruction of a pharaoh and all Egypt by our God.

2Chron 36:20-21, Jer25:11, Dan 9:1-5, Jer 29:10. Israel witnessed his powerful hand of deliverance from the Babylonian captivity at the exact appointed time. They witnessed the fall and destruction of Babylon.

Esther 3:5-15, Esther 7:6-10. Israel witnessed deliverance in the kingdom of Medes and Persians when Yahuwah reversed the plot of the enemy-(Haman) to wipe out the Jews/Judeans.

Joel 3:5-6, 1Maccabees 1:20-64, 2:47-48. Israel witnessed deliverance from the hand of the kingdom of Greece and their plot to scatter Israel and unit everyone to worship as they dictated.

Dan7:17-28, Deut 32:36, Lk21:22-24. Israel witnessed the rise of the fourth wild beast- Rome and the third and final removal of Israel from their Promised Land territory by the Romans in the year AD70. Yes, Israel witnessed the foretold Vengeance and judgment of God on his chosen people because of their errors.

Hos 6:1-2, 2Pt 3:8. Israel was scattered among the nations to bear the 2days =2000 years punishment until it ends.

Hos 6:2, Ezek 37:1-14, Mt 24:32-35. Generation of Israel will witness the raising of the chosen ones/holy ones of Israel from the dead, from among the nations where they were scattered, to their 4th generation or restoration back to the Promised Land (Gen15:16).

Amos 9:11-12, Acts 15:16-18, This generation of Israel that Yahuwah our God will raise up in the final part of the 2days (2000 years) of our punishment will witness the restoring and rebuilding of the booth/ house of David that has fallen or fell in the year AD 70.

Isa 65:8-10, John 6:44, 65. The chosen ones of our God- the offspring of Jacob from among the nations will be witnesses of our God as he fulfills his promise to take out of Jacob and Judah the chosen ones to inherit and take possession of his holy mountain forever.

Isa 46: 8-13, Isa 45:5-7, 17, 21-25, Dan 2:21, Dan 7:21-22, 26-27. This is that we may know that He alone is God and there is no other. He is the one doing all these things. He removes a kingdom and He sets up a kingdom. He gives the ruler ship to the one He has chosen (Ps2:5-12).

Be baptized by the holy spirit of our God.

Mk 1:8. "I baptized you with water, but he will baptize you with the Holy Spirit." John baptized the people of Judea who showed repentance for their sins and errors of the nation with water as a symbol of their repentance. However, he encouraged them to seek for the baptism with the holy spirit of our God by the one to come-Yahushua. Water baptism will not benefit you much without the baptism of the Holy Spirit.

What is the baptism of the Holy Spirit?

It is similar to water baptism. It is the immersion with accurate knowledge, insight, and understanding of our God who is spirit. Water baptism, which is a symbol of repentance and a turning away from dead works, is ok. However, one needs to seek baptism with the Holy Spirit of our God for their salvation.

John 17:3 Acts 11:16, Mk 10:38, Isa 46:3-5, 8-11. Baptism of the Holy Spirit starts with taking in of accurate knowledge of Yahuwah the only true God and his son- Yahushua who He sent.

John 3:7-8. The baptism with the Holy Spirit is given by the spirit of our God that He sends out at appointed times to accomplish His will and decisions about a foretold event.

Baptized in the name of the father, son and Holy Spirit.

Mt 28:19. "Go therefore and make disciples of people of all the nations-(Israelites that will be gathered from among the nations where they were scattered). Baptizing = teaching them with accurate knowledge, understanding, and insight of the name, authority, and power of the father, our God, his Son and the Holy Spirit.

Why?

Hos 4:6. The people of Israel perished for lack of knowledge of their true God, their true messiah, the holy spirit of their God and lack of knowledge of who they are as a people.

Prov 1:23, Isa 8:20. In the final part of the days, these from among the nations will be baptized/taught the name of the father, the Son and the Holy Spirit. That is having accurate knowledge, understanding, and insight as revealed by the words of our God. They will have insight into the activities and works that these are working to accomplish as one from long ago (1John 5:7-8).

Mt 9:17. People do not put new wine in an old wineskin bottle. If they do, the new wine will burst/ overwhelm the old wineskin bottle. The bottle and the new wine will then perish.

In like manner, the Holy Spirit is poured out to the descendants of Jacob who are prepared to receive the Holy Spirit- (new wine or new things of our God) by our God. Those chosen are to receive the gift and help of the spirit in them at the appointed time for a special assignment (John 3:7-8).

Prov1:23, Ps 32:8-9. To receive the gift, first, cleanse yourself of the old wine, and as a new wine bottle be ready to receive the spirit of our God by seeking for the true knowledge, understanding, and insight of the God of Israel.

John 6:44, Isa 54:13. Understand that unless the father chooses you and reveal Himself and His activities to you, you cannot know Him or come to his son to lead you.

Isa 10:20, Isa 8:10-13. Second, cleanse yourself of the old and erroneous ways and teachings about God that we learned from among the nations where we were scattered. Teachings of those who enslaved us and taught us their false religious ways of worshipping (Exod 28:64). This also is only possible with the help of the spirit of God that you receive and is in you (Ezek 36:25, 33).

Hos 6:1. As you seek and earnestly search for Yahuwah the God of Israel to return to Him, He is the one to pour out his holy spirit through his son for you. Then you will grow in accurate knowledge, understanding and insight of him and his activities of long ago (John 14:15-18).

Mt 10:19-20, John 16:13, 1Cor 2:12, 1John 2:27. The Holy Spirit of God that you received will now be the one teaching and guiding you, revealing the things of the father to you through his words. The Spirit will teach you the things the father has done, is doing and will soon do. The things the father wants his chosen ones to do at his appointed times (Mt 4:1, Lk 4:1).

Act2:16-17, Gal 3:26, Gal 4:6, Joel 2:28, Rom 8:14. The holy spirit of our God will from then on lead you, since we receive the spirit of our father through faith in his son into our hearts. We now cry out "Abba Father" as we are led by the spirit of our God.

Baptism and leading by the spirit is like:

John 4:10, 14. Having a source of living water, a spring of water bubbling up from inside of you to impart everlasting life. You will no longer be thirsty again for any other water or go to seek it anywhere else.

John 8:32. It is like having found the truth that sets you free. You do not need to look for it anymore because you found what you have been looking for.

Mt 13:45-46. It is like a merchant looking for the finest pearl. When he found it, he went and sold everything to purchase it. The Holy Spirit leads us to the pearl of high value i.e. accurate knowledge, understanding, and insight into our God and his activities leading us to everlasting life in his promised kingdom.

It is like the loving feeling of newlyweds that continually gets better without fading. You have fallen in love with your understanding of your God, his Son and his Holy Spirit He sends at the appointed time to accomplish his works.

Isa 35:1-10, Isa32:15. It is like a timely rain pour on a desolate wilderness that makes the ground sprout with beautiful plants, flowers, and food for the hungry. The spirit of our God helps us to see what our God is about to accomplish for his chosen ones/ repurchased ones.

Those with faith like that of Abraham, Isaac, and Jacob.

Heb 11:13-14, 1Pt 1:1. They consider themselves as strangers/travelers and foreign residents in the lands where they are presently scattered/residing. They know that they are looking forward to living in a land of their own as promised by our God (Gen 15:13-21).

Heb 11:16, Mt 6:33. Those with faith like Abraham will leave everything of this present world behind to seek a better place/land to come, one belonging to heaven- God's kingdom.

Heb 11:10, 14, Gen 15:16, Dan 2:44, Dan 7:13-14. Those with faith in the God of Abraham, Isaac, and Jacob know and publicly declare that they are waiting for the city and kingdom having a real foundation, whose designer and builder is God.

Gen 15:13-16, Isa 46:8-18, Lk 21:22-24. Those who have faith in Yahuwah the God of Abraham knew that our God's promise to Abraham would be realized/fulfilled in the 4th generation of Abraham's descendants in the Promised Land. It is going to be fulfilled just as our God stated after many nations have enslaved them and taken over their land and scattered them far away to a land that is not theirs.

God's angels will gather back his chosen ones from the four corners of the earth.

Mt 24:31, Mk 13:27. "And he will send out his angels with a great trumpet sound, and they will gather his chosen ones together from the four winds, from one extremity of the heavens to their other extremity.

His angels.

Mt 25:31, Lk1:32-33. The son of man –Yahushua will return in his glory to rule as king over the house of David and all his angels with him.

2Thess 1:7. At the revelation of Yahushua from heaven, with his powerful angels.

Mt 13:39. The reapers/ harvesters are his angels.

Rev 1:1, Rev 12:7, Joel 3:9-16. War will break out in heaven-(ruling governments of this world) versus Yahushua and his angels (Ps 2:1-12).

Mt 13:41. The son of man –Yahushua will send out his angels and they will collect out from his kingdom all things that cause stumbling-(Idols and false gods etc.) and people who practice lawlessness-(doing what you are not permitted or chosen to do and those the kingdom is not promised to).

Ps 103:20. Praise Yahuwah all you his angels, mighty in power, who carry out his word, obeying his voice.

Mt 26:53, Isa 46:8-10. Yahushua will have at his request, God's powerful angels to carry out his will and decisions.

Examples of angelic actions.

Exod 12:29-32. God sent out an angel that killed the entire firstborn of Egypt, both man and animals in 1 night.

Num 20:16, Exod 33:2. It is likely that the angels of our God, ministers who carry out his word executed all the plagues that came upon Egypt. Yes, the credit, praise, and glory belong to our God who is doing all these things known from of old.

Exod 12:21-22. Our God gave protection to Israel using his angels as He led them out of Egypt. A pillar of cloud by day and a pillar of fire by night (Ps 105:39).

Gen 19:1-17. Our God sent two angels to saved Lot and his relatives out of Sodom and Gomorrah and executed his judgment decision concerning that city.

2 Kg 19:35. An angel of Yahuwah killed 185000 Assyrian soldiers in just one night.

Jer 25:29-33, Zech 1:15, Amos 3:6. If one angel of our God can kill a recorded 185000 soldier in just one night, then calculate what Yahushua and a legion of angels with him will do when the time arrives for them to return and execute our God's judgment on the earth. Our God will use his angels also to gather back his scattered chosen ones from four corners of the earth to inherit the Promised Land /kingdom for Abraham's descendants.

Hos 6:1-2, Mt 24:29-31. This He will do immediately after the 2000 years tribulation/punishment on them ends.

Learn from the chief agent/forerunner of our faith.

Heb 2:10, Act 5:31.

Heb 12:2. For the joy set ahead of him, he endured the humiliation and shame from sinners even unto death. Likewise, we in the final part of our punishment and tribulation should consider the joy and glory that will soon be given to the chosen ones of our God in his kingdom to come. To those who endured until the end.

Mt 26:38-46. He persevered in prayer during his final hours of temptation. He submitted to the will of our God. He encouraged us to keep on the watch and to pray continually as we see the end approaching. "Though the spirit is willing to follow through his will to the end, the flesh is weak" when it comes to the temptations of the devil- our adversary.

If we must be victorious over his temptations of our weak fleshly desires, it has to be done through continually being on the watch/lookout for his traps and constantly praying for the help of our father's gift of Holy Spirit to us.

Mk 14:38, Mt 24:4-5. "Keep on the watch and pray continually so that you do not fall into, fall for it or give in to temptation by the devil". The devil will want to mislead us into serving and doing his will and not the will and decisions of our God- our Father in heaven (Mt 6:9).

The temptations by the devil using the desires of men.

1Cor10:13, Deut 8:2, Deut 13:1-4, Ezek 20:31-32, 39, Mt6:13. Every temptation by the devil that comes on us is common to man. Our God is aware of our every temptation by the devil. He will faithfully provide a way to overcome it if we keep asking for His help through continuous prayers to Him.

The desire of the flesh test.

The desire for self-preservation through pursuits of food, housing, clothing, money, and children. The devil will keep tempting us by saying we have to pursue these things to be happy and preserve our lives. Exod 20:1-6, Hos 6:1. Should we leave the most important things to pursue these things?

Mt 4:1-4. Our chief agent did not seek to preserve his own life by satisfying his fleshly desire for food after 40 days of fasting. He knew our lives would be preserved not on food alone but also by obeying every command of our God.

Mt 6:24-34. Our desire for food, shelter, clothing, children, and money can be very strong. However, by watching continually we can avoid being carried away with these desires by the devil and praying for the help of the Holy Spirit we can resist given in to temptation.

Mk10:28-30, 1Jn 2:15, 1Pt 5:9. Yahushua and first-century disciples of our God left everything of these desires to seek first the will/ kingdom of our God and his righteousness. Especially in the final 3.5 years before the next event of the kingdom of heaven.

Amos 9:9, Lk 22: 28-32. Yahushua revealed that all those chosen ones, children of the kingdom of God will be tempted/tested and sifted as wheat to see if they have faith in the God of Abraham and his promise of a kingdom.

Mt 7:13-14, Lk 22:28, 33, Mk 10:38-39. The road/gate back to the kingdom is tough and rough, only a few will walk in it or follow it back to the kingdom. Those who stuck with their chief agent and savior until the end.

Jer 31:16-21, Acts 1:7. Those who set up road markers or signposts to know when the time to return back to the kingdom is near.

The desire for prominence, fame, wealth, education/degrees of this world.

Mk 9:34-37, Mk 10:35-40. The devil will tempt all chosen ones for the kingdom with these desires for self-important and fame to see if they will sacrifice the pursuit of the kingdom for these vainglories in this world.

Mt 4:8-10. The chief agent of our faith rejected all these desires but chose to render sacred service to our God and do his will. We too should keep on the watch to avoid sacrificing all our lives pursuing/seeking these desires. Praying continuously for the help of the Holy Spirit will help us avoid falling into these temptations of the devil. Only then are we able to keep seeking first his kingdom and the will of our God now as his kingdom draws near.

Rendering of sacrifice/service test.

Mt 4:5-7, Ezek 20:39-43. We cannot serve two masters at the same time. We cannot obey the voice of Satan and the voice of our God at the same time. Yahushua stated that our obedient belong to our God, and to him alone we are to render our sacred service in his holy mountain.

Hos 6:1-2, Lk 1:69-75. We have almost used up the time-(2000 years) given to us to serve the devil's will. It is now time to seek and return to our God and render sacred service to him alone in his holy mountain in Zion.

Ps 40:8, Heb10:7-9, Rev 6:2, 2Thess 1:6-10.The chief agent of our faith summited to doing the will of our God and to render sacred service to him alone. He will return at the appointed time to complete his conquest/victory over the devil.

Rev 6:11, Mt 24:9. Likewise, if we endure until the end and not give in to the devil's tempting offers we will be victorious over the devil and his world.

Yahuwah's loyal love for Israel will endure forever.

Ps 136:1-26, Lam 3:22, Ps 100:5.

1. Give thanks to Yahuwah, for he is good: His loyal love endures forever.
2. Give thanks to the God of gods: For his loyal love endures forever.
3. Give thanks to the Lord of lords: For his loyal love endures forever.
4. He alone does great wonders: For his loyal love endures forever.
5. He skillfully made the heavens: For his loyal love endures forever.
6. He spread out the earth over the waters: For his loyal love endures forever.
7. He made the great lights: For his loyal love endures forever.
8. The sun to rule over the day: For his loyal love endures forever.
9. The moon and the stars to rule over the night: For his loyal love endures forever.
10. He struck down Egypt's firstborn: For his loyal love endures forever.
11. He brought Israel out from their midst: For his loyal love endures forever.
12. With a mighty hand and an outstretched arm: For his loyal love endures forever.

13. He split the Red Sea in two: For his loyal love endures forever.

14. He caused Israel to pass through the middle of it: For his loyal love endures forever.

15. He shook off Pharaoh and his army into the Red Sea: For his loyal love endures forever.

16. He led his people through the wilderness: For his loyal love endures forever.

17. He struck down great kings: For his loyal love endures forever.

18. He killed mighty kings: For his loyal love endures forever.

19. Si'hon the king of the Amorites: For his loyal love endures forever.

20. And Og the king of Bashan: For his loyal love endures forever.

21. He gave their land as an inheritance: For his loyal love endures forever.

22. An inheritance to Israel his servant: For his loyal love endures forever.

23. He remembered us when we were low: For his loyal love endures forever.

24. He kept rescuing us from our adversaries: For his loyal love endures forever.

25. He gives food to every living thing: For his loyal love endures forever.

26. Give thanks to the God of the heavens: For his loyal love endures forever.

He will have mercy and pardon our errors (Isa 14:1-3): For his loyal love endures forever.

He will gather back his inheritance- Israel (Mt 24:29-31): For his loyal love endures forever.

He will give the nations in exchange for his people (Isa 43:3): For his loyal love endures forever.

The waters and the rivers will not swallow up Israel (Isa 43:2): For his loyal love endures forever.

The fire will not scorch nor the flame singe Israel (Isa 43:2): For his loyal love endures forever.

He will come to our aid in the morning (Isa 37:36, Ps 30:5): For his loyal love endures forever.

The remnant of Israel will possess the land He promised (Gen 15:16): For his loyal love endures forever.

He will set up on it an offspring of David to rule forever (Lk 1:32-33): For his loyal love endures forever.

He will never uproot Israel again from the land (Amos 9:15): For his loyal love endures forever.

He will watch over Israel for good and not for bad (John 17:15, Jer 31:10, 28): For his loyal love endures forever.

No weapon directed against Israel will succeed (Isa 54:17): For his loyal love endures forever.

Great and wonderful things our God has done and will do for us (Rev 15:3, Job9:10, Isa 28:29, Job 5:9): For his loyal love endures forever.

Let all creation praise our God: For his loyal love endures forever.

Let the repurchased ones of our God praise him (Isa 43:1): For his loyal love endures forever.

Praise Yahuwah our God in Zion (Isa 46:13): For his loyal love will endure forever.

Yahushua stated that all those that came in place of Him are thieves and plunderers of the sheep.

John 10:7-9. So Jesus said again: "Most truly I say to you, I am the door for the sheep. 8 All those who have come in place of me are thieves and plunderers, but the sheep have not listened to them. 9 I am the door; whoever enters through me will be saved, and that one will go in and out and find pasturage".

Dan 9:25. Before the arrival of the messiah the leader, many arose proclaiming themselves as the leader and savior of Israel- God's sheep. However, Yahushua said that they are all thieves and plunderers that have come in place of him. The true sheep of Israel have not listened to them or followed them.

John 10:11, 14-15. Yahushua is the foretold fine shepherd to gather and shepherd God's sheep-Israel. Ezek 11-15, Amos 9:11-15, Mt24:29-31. Yahushua the leader will lead in the gathering of the scattered sheep of Israel from among the nations and rebuilding of the house of David that fell in year A.D.70.

Mt 24:4-6, 24. In answer, Jesus said to them: "Look out that nobody misleads you, 5 for many will come based on my name, saying, 'I am the Christ,' and will mislead many. 6 You are going to hear of wars and reports of wars. See that you are not alarmed, for these things must take place, but the end is not yet". As was in the days before the arrival of the messiah the leader, many thieves and plunders has arisen to mislead and draw away many sheep of the house of Israel. The plunderers want the sheep to follow them and not wait for their chief fine shepherd to return from heaven to do the gathering (John 15:6). These sheep are being misled because they are following men instead of searching out from the written confirmation the voice of the fine shepherd. The thieves and plunderers do not really know where to lead the sheep to, so they led them to their destruction=fire.

Yahushua stated, "My sheep will hear my voice and listen to me".

Isaiah 8:16. "Wrap up the written confirmation; Seal up the law among my disciples! ".

John 15:5-7, Mt 13:11. First-century disciples, sheep of our God listened and followed the fine shepherd. They observed his words and followed his directions regarding the next scheduled event concerning the nation of Israel.

John 10:16, Dan 12:2-4. The other sheep of Israel, Final day's disciples of our God, likewise will listen to the voice of the fine shepherd, observe, and follow his directions until he returns to gather all his sheep back to their homeland.

Following these men leads to destruction.

Isaiah 8:7-12. Yes, following the conspiracy voice of invaders, enemies of the sheep of Israel, The pope, the bishops, Governing body, Reverend fathers, pastors, imams, and elder of different religious organizations instead of the voice of the fine shepherd will lead to the destruction of any sheep of Israel. These men are not leading the sheep of Israel to their foretold destination (Isaiah 46:13, Zech 8:1-8, Rev 21:3-4) rather to a different destination where they will be slaughtered in wars (Isaiah10:21-23, Amos 9:10).

Mt 24:6-7, Joel 3:2-12, Rev 16:16. Religious wars – holy wars, Wars of the nations, the war of Armageddon, the war of God and the nations.

There remains a Sabbath day rest for the chosen ones of our God.

Heb 4:8-9. "For if Joshua had led them into a place of rest, God would not afterward have spoken of another day. Therefore, there remains a Sabbath rest for the people of God.

Why?

Gen 15:13-16. Joshua indeed led the Israelites to possess the Promised Land, however, Israel will have no rest in the land is the prophetic utterance of the true God to Abraham until Israel's 4th generation in the Promised Land. In the 1st century, days of the messiah and apostles, Israel was in their 3rd generation in their possession of the Promised Land.

Dan 9:26, Lk 22:20-24, Mt 24:2, Isa 26:12-13, 18. The land was destroyed and desolated by the Romans, the 4th wild beast foretold to come upon the land promised to Abraham's descendant-Israel. Israel is yet to possess the Promised Land for the 4th generation or fourth time.

Lk 1:32-33, Dan 2:44, Rev11:18 Rev 20:6. Israel will enjoy 1000 years of peace and rest in the Promised Land when they possess it for the fourth time.

*When will the fourth generation of Israel
return to possess the Promised Land forever?*

Mt 24:29-31, Isa 26:20, Dan 12:7. Immediately after
the tribulation /punishment for the error of Israel
ends.

Hos 6:1-2, 2Pt 3:8, Isa 10:21-23. After the 2days
(2000 years) punishment ends, the chosen ones of
Israel will be restored on the 3rd day =1000 years
Sabbath day rest from all our tribulations.

Isa 46:8-10, Acts 15:17-18, Amos 9:11-12. All
praises and glory of the kingdom belong to our God
who foretold and has continued to work to bring to
fulfillment the things He foretold long ago.

The lord/king of the Sabbath day.

Mk 2:28, Lk 1:32-33, John 10:1-9. Yahushua, the son
of man is the lord or king of the Sabbath day rest for
the chosen ones of Israel. Then He will rule as king
over the house of David forever and shepherd the
sheep of God.

Do whatever possible to enter his rest.

Heb 4:11, Mt 6:33, Mt 7:13-14, Mt 5:30. Now that you
know, what the Sabbath day rest is and when it will
come, do whatever possible to enter his rest. Do not
let lack of faith in the promises of our God or

disobedience to his laws and commands cause you not to enter his rest.

Exo 20:5, Deut 28:64, Ezek 20:32, John 4:22-24. He commands that we worship Him alone and have no other gods among us. We should not follow the nations/ peoples to serve their gods and idols (Christianity, Islam, Buddhism, etc.).

Deut 30:1-8, Hos 6:1. Now is a favorable time that we turn around and return, seek and worship Yahuwah our God with spirit and truth if we are going to enter His rest.

Rev 18:4-5, Isa 48:20, Isa 52:11, Jer 50:8, Mt 6:4. Stay away or flee from all erected religious high places of false worship among the nations-(Babylon the great). Call on your God in the secret places of your house with your family members who are seeking the true God. Yahuwah who sees in secret will hear and deliver you and give you his rest at the appointed time.

What separates one Israelite person from another? What separates one of Abraham's offspring from another? What separates a chosen Israelite for God's rest from the gentile -peoples of the nations?

The blood, skin color or physical appearance, the status in life or level of education does not separates and identify one as a true chosen one to serve and worship the God of Israel. The spirit and the knowledge of the true God are what separates.

The spirit.

John 4:24, Mic 4:5, Isa 10:21-23, Rom 9:27-28. Each race of people receives and operates by the spirit of their gods. The spirit in one determines and regulates how you live your life and conduct your reverential fears. Israelites who keep rejecting his spirit He will reject and obstinate.

Deut 7:6, Deut 14:2, Amos 3:2, John 6:44, 65, Isa 65:8-10. God will choose his chosen ones to serve and worship him as God.

Prov 1:23, Acts 2:17-18, 38-39, John 14:16-17, Rom8:16, Ps 147:19-20. Yahuwah will pour out the Holy Spirit for his chosen ones to worship Him. The world- (gentile nations) cannot receive this spirit of truth or knowledge of what it is accomplishing.

Knowledge of the true name of God.

Exo 3:13-15, John 17:17, Acts 2:21-22. God reveals his true name and activities only to his chosen ones of Israel for them to call on Him for their salvation. Amos 3:7. He reveals what He is doing to his chosen prophets of Israel.

Hos 4:6. The rest of Israel without knowledge of their God will perish for lack of knowledge.

Ps 147:19-20, John 4:22. Other peoples and nations do not know or understand the activities and judgments of the only true God- God of Israel.

What name are you calling on for your salvation?

Allah, God, Lord, Elohim, Yahweh, Yahuah, Yahuwah, Jehovah, Jesus Christ, Yahusha, Yahushua, etc.?
The nations invented and profaned the name of the true God. However, the true God will make his name known to His chosen ones. They will call on his name for their salvation.

The spirit that the chosen ones receive which is in
them will teach each one the name of the father to
call on.

On whom does God put/pours out his spirit?

Joel 2:28-29, Lk 1:69-75. He pours out his spirit on his chosen male and female servants. Those that our God will choose to render sacred service to Him at the appointed times of events of the last days.

Who has Yahuwah chosen as his servants?

Is it every one of every race? No.

Rom 9:4-5, Act 26:7. Sacred service to Yahuwah belongs to the Israelites -12 tribes.
Why?

Deut 7:6, 14:2, Isa 41:8, Isa 45:4, Jer 30:10, Isa 44:21, Isa 49:3, Isa 44:1, Jer 46:27-28. God chose Israel out of all the peoples/races on earth to serve as his special property. They are his servants from generation to generation. The people He has used and will use to declare his splendor on earth.

Why then is everyone (other races) now claiming to be servant or spokesperson for God?

Dan 8: 4-12, 19-26, 2Thess 2:3-5. It was foretold that a man of lawlessness – (a people) would come and bring in apostasy and desolation. They will cause many to fall away from what is written and revealed in the scriptures (Deut 7:6,14:2, Isa 41:8, Rom 9:4).

Who are these people- (the man of lawlessness)?

Dan 8:4-12. A people liken to a male goat that wants to rape everything and sow its own seed. A people that can cross the surface of the earth without touching the ground (flying or sailing).

Dan 8:19-26. This man of lawlessness started to come into the holy place to take it over starting with the Greek kingdom and continued to the Romans kingdom and their descendants today in places of worship.

Dan 8:10-12, Dan 9:26, 2Thess 2:3-5. They will act lawlessly, throwing the truth to the ground/earth. They will have success destroying, changing everything and exalting themselves above every so-called god or object of worship. They will take over and preside over places of worship, showing their image as a god (e.g. white Jesus) and themselves as servant /spokesperson.

2Thess 2:3, 9-12, Rev 12:9. They will mislead the entire inhabited earth except those whose names are in the book of life- (Israelites marked for salvation).

Dan 8:13-14. For 2300 evenings and mornings = 2300 days.

Ezek 4:6, Num 14:34. Apply a day for a year for the sins of Israel. 2300 days =2300 years.

Lk 21:24. This trampling by the lawless one will continue until the appointed time- (2300 years) is fulfilled.

It elapsed 300 years to end of Greek civilization to the rise of Roman world power/civilization until 2000 years has ended.

Is the 2300 years punishment/ sentence too long for the chosen race-Israel?

Deut 32:16-27. Vs 26-27. It could have been more or worse, but then no flesh will be saved. However, because of the chosen ones to receive the mercy of our God, the days are cut short to 2300 years punishment (Mt 24:22, Mk 13:20, Dan 8:13-14). This 2300 years trampling of the holy place –Jerusalem will start with the kingdom of Greece and will extend to the rise of the Roman kingdom and its remnants.

Dan 8:14, Mt 24:29-31. After which the holy place will certainly be restored to its former glory.
John 8:32. Yahushua said "You will know the truth and the truth will set you free"

God will awaken Israel and pour out His spirit on them in the final part of the 2300 years trampling.

Ezek 37:1-14, John 5:28-29. God will awaken by pouring out his spirit on the whole house of Israel in the final part of the 2300 days.

John 6:44, 65, Isa 65:8-10. The chosen ones will then be gathered back to the land (the kingdom).

John 14:26, Isa 59:21, Prov 1:23, Lk 1:69-75. The spirit that they received seals the chosen ones.

Isa 10:21-23, Ezek 20:36-38, Amos 9:10. The rest will be destroyed.

None of the chosen ones will fall to the ground without our father's notice.

John 6:44, 65. Unless the father chooses a person, He or she cannot come to know the father or come to the son.

John 17:12. The chosen ones are guided and protected on account of our father's name.
Why?
Isa 65:8-10. They are to inherit his holy mountain-Zion.
Isa 43:1-10. They are to be witnesses of our God's actions that He will perform.
Isa 41:8. They are to serve as His servants.

Examples.

Isa 42:1, Acts3:19. Yahushua, a chosen one was safely guided and is being safeguarded until the appointed time for restoration of all things to him.

Nehemiah 2:5-8. Nehemiah a chosen one was safely guided and given favor and protection to accomplish Yahuwah's will.

John 17:12. The chosen disciples and apostles were safely guided and protected.

Mt 6:26-32. If you are one of His chosen ones, do not worry or be anxious. Our father will take care of things. He knows what you need to accomplish your assignment and will supply them at the appointed time.

The help of our father's Holy Spirit.

Joel 2:28-29, John 14:26. Our God promised to pour out the help of His holy spirit on His chosen ones in the last days of every event that He has foretold will take place.

Prov 1:23, John 14:16-17. His spirit will teach and make the words of our God known to the chosen ones.

Acts 2:38-39, Ezek 39:29, Isa 44:3. The promised Holy Spirit is for the descendants of Israel that our God will choose or call to himself to be His witnesses and servants in the final days before the new thing He is doing.

No nation will endure Yahuwah's denunciation and judgment.

Jer 10:10. "Yahuwah is the true God and eternal king. The earth will quake because of his indignation. No nation will endure his indignation".

His judgment decisions.

Deut 32:36, 1Pt 4:17, 1Cor 11:32. His judgment started first with his people-Israel; Thereafter, His judgment will come to other nations. Israel is first to receive His judgment so that not all Israel is destroyed with the rest of the world.
Deut 32:36, Amos 9:1-8, Isa 65:8-10, Isa 46:3, 8, Act15:14-18. God will have mercy and save a remnant of Israel his people after first judging them.

His Judgment decisions on Israel.

Isa 26:20, 8, Lk 21:22, 24, Mt24:2. Israel will enter and follow His judgment path until it ends. It will be a day of meting out justice/punishment on Israel to fulfill all the things written (Hos 7:12, Deut 28:15-68).

Dan 8:13-14, Num 14:34, Lam 5:2. The Gentile nations will trample Jerusalem and the holy place for and appointed time of 2300 years.

Hos 6:1-2, 5, 2Pt 3:8. For 2days = 2000 years of this judgment, Israel will be judged in the wilderness-among the nations (Hos 2:14, Hos 3:4-5, Hos 5:15, Amos 9:9-10, Deut 28:64, Hos 9:16-17).

Jer 10:10. Israel will cease to exist during these 2000 years because no nation will endure His denunciation.

His judgment decisions on other nations.

Deut 32:35, 37. Yahuwah has judgment stored up for other nations too. It will take place after His punishment on Israel ends.

Deut 32:41-43, Isa 34:8. He will judge the nations for what they have done to his people.

Mic 1:3-5, Jer 25:25-38, 2Pt 2:9, 3:7-12. His judgment will be intense and nothing will escape it.

Jer 10:10, 1Pt 4:17-19, Heb 10:31, Ezek 39:21-29. No nation will endure his denunciation. Ask the Israelites they will tell you. It is a fearful thing to come under His judgment.

How death will be no more.

Rev 21:3-4. "The house /dwelling place of God will be among his people. He will wipe out tears from their eyes and death will be no more, neither will mourning nor outcry nor pain be anymore. The former things have passed away".

Hos 5:15, Hos 6:1-2, Hos 3:4-5, Ps 83:12. Our God abandoned Israel, his people and went back to heaven so that people of Israel will bear the punishment for all their sins.
Exo 20:5, Ezek 18:4, Rom 3:23, Rom 6:23. The wages of sin is death. Since all Israel has sinned, the nation and its people were put to death or cease to exist as a punishment for their error.

Examples.

Gen 19:24, Jude 7, 2Pt 2:6. Cities of Sodom and Gomorrah received the judgment of death. They were destroyed with fire and ceased to exist because of their gross sins.

2Pt 2:5, Gen 7:11.The ancient world of Noah's day was destroyed by the flood and ceased to exist because of their sins.

Jer 10:10. The judgment result of ignoring the righteous laws of God on any people is death.

Deut 32:32-38, Dan 2:44, Dan 8:25, Isa 45:6-7, Isa 46:8-10. Long ago, God foretold death for Israel and death for other nations at the appointed times. Nevertheless, it will start with Israel first.

Israel's death and resurrection.

Deut 32:20, 26, 36, Ezek 37:1-14, Isa 14:1-3, Zech8:1-8. True People of Israel will become like dead and forgotten people in all the nations. They will be cut off from the inheritance (land) that God gave to them. However, God will have mercy on the whole house of Israel and will resurrect /awaken them in the final part of the days of their punishment. Gen 15:16, Ezek 39:21-29. God will restore Israel back to the land He promised to give to their ancestor Abraham as a lasting possession.

Death will be no more.

Hos 6:1-2, Rev 21:4, Isa 25:8. After Israel's resurrection and restoration, death will no more occur to the nation and the people of Israel.

Mt 1:21, Lk 1:32-32, 69-75, John 5:25-29, John 11:25, Mt 24:29-31. Yahushua is the means for resurrecting Israel and the people back to life. Those who have listened and understood the message will live, for the others, it will be a resurrection for a second death (Isa10:21-23, Amos 9:10-11, Ezek 20:36-38).

Death judgment for the other nations.

Deut 32:39-43, Mic 5:15, Jer25:32-33, Amos 9:12. The judgment of other nations will start after Israel's judgment ends. Yahuwah will war with the nations and those put to death by our God will be many on that day.

Dan 2:44, Jer 10:10, Joel 3:1-10, Lam 2:1, 17, Lam 1:21 Rev 12:17. No nation will endure God's denunciation. Therefore, these nations will cease to exist, destroyed as was in the days of Noah, Sodom and Gomorrah and ancient nation of Israel.

People of Israel will find favor in the wilderness.

Jer 31:1-2, Ezek 39:21-29. "At that time," declares Yahuwah, "I will become God to all the families of Israel, and they will become my people." This is what Yahuwah says: "The people who survived the sword found favor in the wilderness When Israel was walking to his resting-place."

Why the sword on Israel?

Deut 32:16-29, Amos 9:1-10, Mt 23:37-39. Israel provoked their God, the living God to anger; He then unleashed the sword after the people of Israel.

The sin of Israel is that they abandoned their God and started following and worshiping inferior gods of the nations.

Amos 3:1-2, Amos 9:7-9, Isa 45:11-13. Yahuwah has a relationship with only the people of Israel and will, therefore, punish them for all their errors. He can identify them wherever they are hiding and will execute his decision to annihilate the sinners among them when the time comes. They are like the Cushite's-(Ethiopians) who are of African, dark race.

Where is the wilderness?

Jer 31:2, Amos 9:8-9. "Those who survived the sword of Yahuwah found favor in the wilderness".

Ezek 20:34-38, Ezek 39:21-24, Lk 21:24. The wilderness is among the peoples/ nations where Israel was scattered to bear judgment and punishment for all their errors until the annihilation time for sinners of Israel (Mt 10:21-22).

When will the annihilation occur?

Isa 10:21-23, Amos 9:9-15. Towards the end of the 2days =2000 years punishment among the nations, before the gathering of the chosen ones back to the kingdom of their father.

Deut 32:36, Ezek 36:22-30, Ezek 39:21, 27-28. Our God will sanctify His name that Israel profaned among the nations where Israel has gone. He will display His power to destroy the wicked/ sinners while salvaging the humbled and righteous ones among His people.

Isa 14:1-3, Ezek 20:40-42, Amos 9:1-5, Mt 24:29-31.Those who escaped the sword (judgment) of destruction that our God unleashed on his people - Israel will find mercy and favor in the wilderness of the peoples. They will be collected back to serve their God in the kingdom territory He promised

Abraham and his chosen off springs to inherit forever (Gen15:16).

Let Him that has understanding pay attention to what the spirit of Yahuwah has revealed.

Deut 6:7. Israel we received instruction to teach the true knowledge and laws of Yahuwah our God to our children for them to observe and obey. We until today have not obeyed the voice of Yahuwah. Rather we chose to teach sports and the ways of the nations to our children.

Deut 28:64, Ezek 20:32. Israel our sin is leaving our God and serving the gods of other nations. For this sin, all who refuse to turn around and return to serve their God will all be destroyed (Isa 10:21-23).

Dan 8:13-14, Mt 11:12. For our refusing to obey the voice of Yahuwah, Our God subjected the land territory He gave to our ancestors and us to inherit to desolation and trampling by gentile nations until 2300 years have passed.

Hos 3:4-5, Hos 6:1-2, 2Pt3:8, Lk 21:22, 24. For 2days = 2000 years of this punishment /tribulation, Israel will be displaced, scattered people and will dwell among other nations.

Deut 30:1-8, Prov1:23, Isa 43:1-8, Mt 24:29-31. Israel our God asked us to choose life that we and our children may live. He promised to save us and gather us from the ends of the earth.

Exod 20:5, 2Cor 3:7-11, Jer 31:31-38. The end of the old covenant made with our ancestors is now near the end of its 2300 years trampling and punishment stage. It has 13 years more from the year 2020 before it will be removed completely and replaced with a new covenant.

Hos 6:1, Prov 1:23. Accept the discipline and humiliation from our God and return to Him by confessing our sins of serving other gods (Deut 28:64), and then He will make his words known to us.

Isa 46:3-5, 8-11, Isa 10:21-23, Amos 9:1, 10, Ezek 20:38. The sinners and those of Israel without faith, those who are thinking that Yahuwah will not carry out what He foretold long ago will all see their end.

The conclusion of the matter.

The conclusion of the matter is this; Yahuwah the God of Israel, the only living God will be exalted as king and God overall. His name will be sanctified by the display of His powers at His appointed times to execute all that is His will.

The kingdom territory He promised to give to the chosen ones of Abraham's off springs will be fulfilled. It will be restored and rebuild by the chosen king and ruler of God's people –Yahushua at his return.

The remaining ones of all the nations will be subject to the ruler ship in Zion. Israel will enjoy Yahuwah's protection and blessings for a long time. Let Israel wait on Yahuwah. Praise yah you people.

You can contact the author with any inquiry at taladi3@gmail.com.

About The Author

Thomas O. Aladi, is from Urualla, Ideato North Local Government Imo State, Nigeria. He sojourned to USA in 1999. He attended Three Rivers Community College Missouri USA, where He studied business administration and then attended Norfolk State University where he studied and earned BSC degree in Electronic Technology Engineering in 2003.

From early childhood I was very interested in the bible and the stories it presented, fascinated on God and His dealings with human race especially the ones he chose to serve him. Throughout my school years the deep desire to understand God kept motivating my search for truth in religion and the bible.

The search for understanding and knowledge of the true God led me to write and share the knowledge that only the Holy Spirit sent from above can reveal.

I view myself and others as traveling merchants searching for the finest pearl –scriptural truth that will set us free from years of being misled away by the wicked from the real truth of our God's revealed words. Thanks to our God for fulfilling his promise to pour out his spirit on us in the last days of our tribulations in order to make his words known to us.

My first book, The Road leading back to Zion; Homecoming for chosen off springs of Abraham is written with intentions to reacquaint humankind with the true knowledge of God and his activities of long   ago.

All can be liberated by accurate understanding of what is written down in the bible if they are willing to search for the knowledge stored in the books and seek the help of the God behind the things written. The second book, "Extra Oil For Your Lamps; As You Wait For The Master's Return" will be a step up in understanding and clarifications of what the true God is revealing by means of His spirit using his words.

This third book, "Follow the Light of Truth Back to Zion; Your Word Is Truth" is written to strengthen and encourage the chosen ones who will inherit the promises of our God, to endure in the hope until the end of His appointed time. Our God is able to restore us to the land if we keep moving on His righteous side by having our faith in Him.

www.ingramcontent.com/pod-product-compliance
Lightning Source LLC
Chambersburg PA
CBHW051104050726

47592CB00002B/664